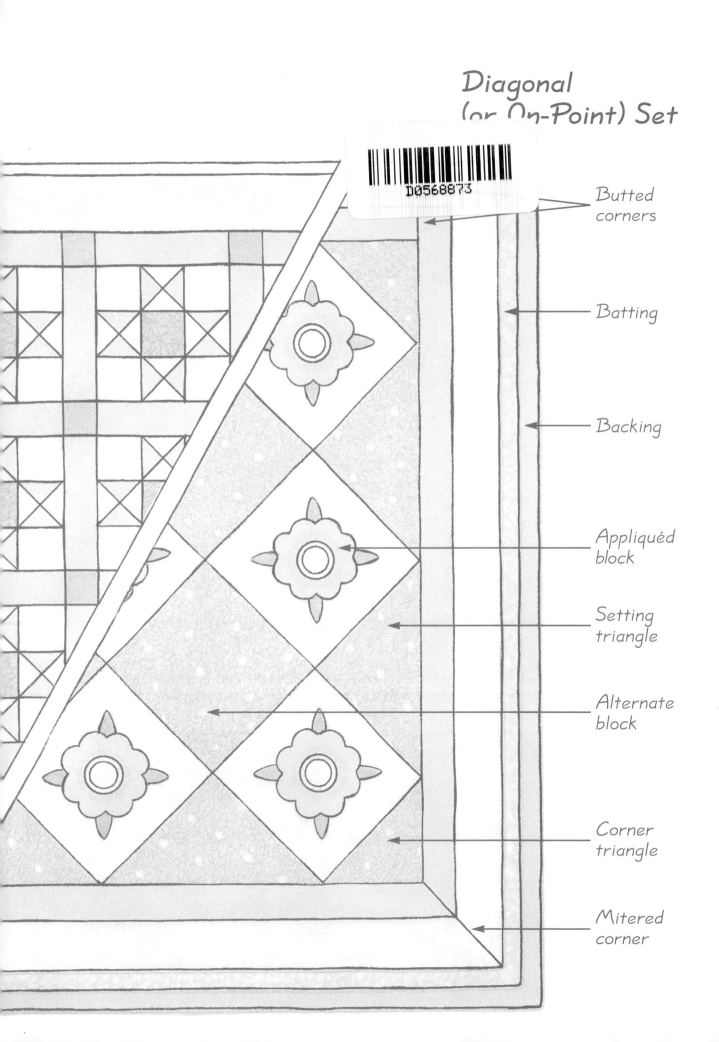

Diagonal (or On-Point) Set

Butted corners

Batting

Backing

Appliquéd block

Setting triangle

Alternate block

Corner triangle

Mitered corner

Rodale's Successful Quilting Library®

Creative Embellishments

Darra Duffy Williamson
Editor

RODALE

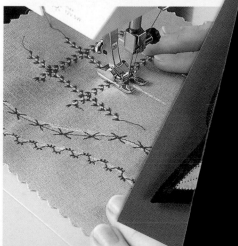

RODALE

WE **INSPIRE** AND **ENABLE** PEOPLE TO IMPROVE
THEIR LIVES AND THE WORLD AROUND THEM

The writers and editors who compiled this book have tried to make all of the contents as accurate and as correct as possible. Illustrations, photographs, and text have all been carefully checked and cross-checked. However, due to the variability of personal skill, tools, materials, and so on, neither the writers nor Rodale Inc. assumes any responsibility for any injuries suffered or for damages or other losses incurred that result from the material presented herein. All instructions should be carefully studied and clearly understood before beginning any project.

Printed in the United States of America on acid-free ∞ , recycled paper ♻

We're always happy to hear from you.

For questions or comments concerning the editorial content of this book, please write to:

Rodale Inc.
Book Readers' Service
33 East Minor Street
Emmaus, PA 18098

Look for other Rodale books wherever books are sold. Or call us at (800) 848-4735.

For more information about Rodale and the books and magazines we publish, visit our Web site at:
www.rodale.com

On the cover: Detail, A Bird in the Hand, by Polly Whitehorn
On these pages: Power Surge, by Ginette Bourque
On the Contents pages: Coral Reef, by Carol Taylor

Book Producer: Eleanor Levie,
    Craft Services, LLC
Art Director: Lisa J. F. Palmer
Editor: Darra Duffy Williamson
Writers: Karen Kay Buckley, Laura Heine, Diane Herbort, Alice Allen Kolb, Diana Leslie, Linda McGehee, Karen Phillips-Shwallon, Diane Rode Schneck, Elizabeth Rosenberg, Janet Rostocki, Jan Smiley, Susan L. Stein, and Carol Taylor
Photographer: John P. Hamel
Illustrator: Mario Ferro
Copy and Photo Editor: Erana Bumbardatore
Indexer: Nan N. Badgett
Hand Model: Melanie Sheridan

Rodale Inc.
Editorial Manager, Rodale's Successful
    Quilting Library: Ellen Pahl
Studio Manager: Leslie M. Keefe
Layout Designer: Keith Biery
Product Manager: Daniel Shields
Product Specialist: Jodi Schaffer
Series Designer: Sue Gettlin

Library of Congress Cataloging-in-Publication Data published the first volume of this series as:

Rodale's successful quilting library.
    p.   cm.
Includes index.
    ISBN 0–87596–760–4 (hc: v. 1:alk paper)
    1. Quilting. 2. Patchwork. I. Soltys, Karen
Costello. II. Rodale Press.
TT835.R622 1997
746.46'041—dc21   96–51316

Creative Embellishments
    ISBN 1–57954–332–4 hardcover

**Distributed to the book trade
by St. Martin's Press**

4 6 8 10 9 7 5 3   hardcover

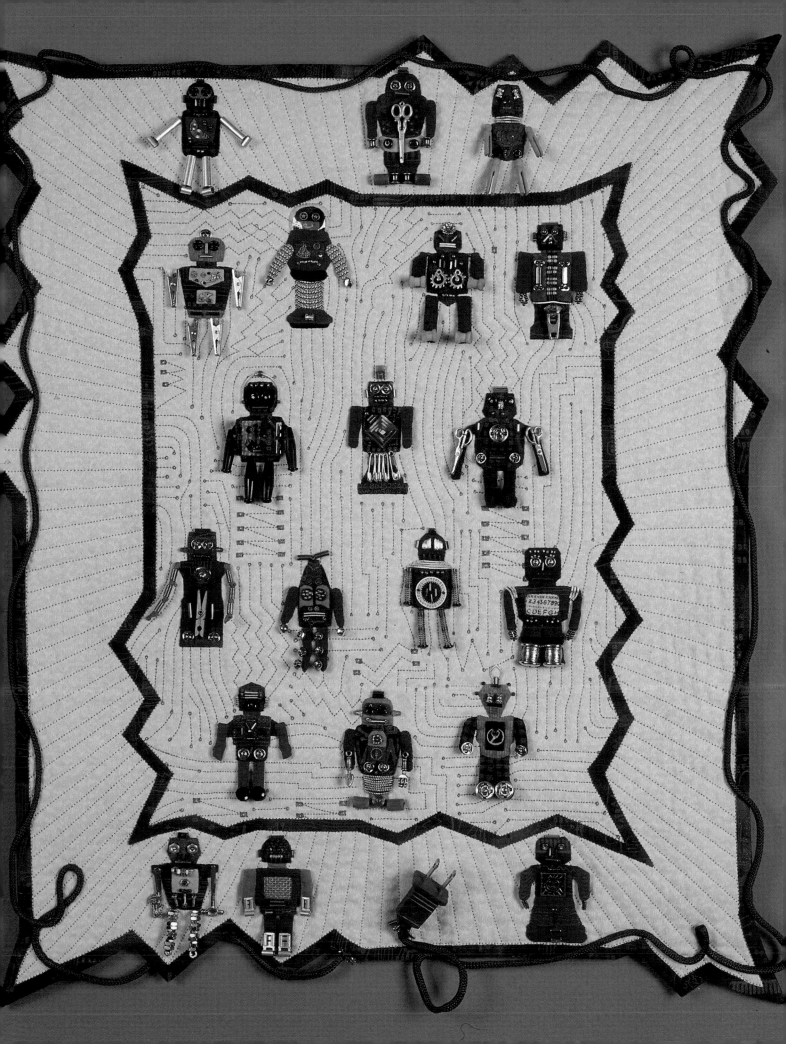

Contents

Introduction

I confess: I have been leading a double life. For years, traditionally inspired scrap quilts defined the face I revealed to the quilting world. Meanwhile, behind the closed doors of my sewing room, I harbored a secret passion for embellishment. It began innocently enough with a passing attraction to the tempting array of beads, buttons, and threads available at quilt shows and craft and fabric stores. Almost before I realized it, though, my collection of trinkets and trims was rivaling my fabric stash. Embellishment is seductive, and I had definitely fallen under its spell!

About this same time, I began quietly exploring less-traditional ways of working, creating quilts that—to my mind, at least—were much more receptive to my various "doodads." But like a child who won't let the mashed potatoes touch the string beans, I kept my embellishing experiments a safe distance from my more traditional work. Then one day I had a revelation. Why *couldn't* I have the best of both worlds—that is, incorporate my "guilty pleasures" into the blocks and appliqués of my more traditional quilts as well? I tried it, and it worked!

That very flexibility is a major focus of this book. Whatever your personal style or taste in quiltmaking, you can indulge yourself guiltlessly in the pleasures of embellishment! Of course, we aim not only to inspire, but also to show you *how*, so we've called upon a cadre of world-class embellishers to share their techniques and tips for picture-perfect results.

Handwork aficionados will delight in Karen Phillips-Shwallon's embroidery methods, while those who prefer to work by machine will stitch under the expert guidance of Alice Allen Kolb. Laura Heine reveals her method for creating lacy threadwork appliqués, Linda McGehee unravels the mystique of pintucks, Jan Smiley introduces playful rubber stamps, and Elizabeth Rosenberg shares her easy-going approach to couching! In short, whether you wish to add a single button or a thousand bugle beads, you'll find all the information you need tucked into these pages.

Should your inclination be toward the elegant and feminine, you're sure to be captivated by the delicate ribbons and silky braids Karen Kay Buckley uses to create her dimensional floral fantasies. Gaga over glamour? Wait until you see what Diane Rode Schneck has in store in her chapter, "Puttin' on the Glitz." Luminous lamés; sparkly spangles, studs, and shishas; glitzy threads, trims, and fabric paints all shine there. And high-tech quilters will want to check out the intriguing hardware and recyclables such as metallic mesh, washers, nuts, zippers, and so forth that Diane Herbort suggests in "Innovative Trimmings."

If you have a particular agenda, embellishment offers a viable and exciting opportunity for carrying it out. As Carol Taylor demonstrates, you can use it to create mood and atmosphere (under the sea or elsewhere) in your quilts. Susan Stein suggests it as a wonderful option for defining a focal point or as creative first aid for a less-than-lovely project. Diana Leslie shows how embellishment can play a role in designing a memory quilt, and you'll be amazed by Janet Rostocki's bag of tricks that add creative touches to sashings and the edges of quilts.

In addition to that amazing lineup of experts, we wanted this volume to offer a little something extra. So we provided six of our experts with the same basket block, and we gave them free rein. (It looked like so much fun, I just had to join in!) See the results of our challenge, starting on page 114.

One final "footnote" on the allure of embellishment: Well into editing this book, I fell and broke my foot. I was outfitted with a pair of crutches and a stiff, thick-soled, decidedly unattractive mesh shoe. As I sat at the computer, foot propped awkwardly on a chair beside me, I found my gaze wandering more and more often to that shoe. When I caught myself plotting how I might spruce it up

with beads, embroidery, glittery trims, and fabric paint, I knew my surrender to embellishment was complete! I have no doubt you'll fall under embellishment's spell just as I have. My best advice? Give in to temptation…and enjoy every moment!

Happy embellishing,

Darra Duffy Williamson

Darra Duffy Williamson
Editor

1 Sort identical shank-style buttons onto extra-large safety pins for storage. You'll know in an instant—and without digging through your entire button box—whether you have enough of one kind of button before starting a new project. Sort sew-through buttons the same way, or string them onto a strong thread, such as buttonhole twist.

2 Wash, dry, and then reuse empty spice jars or used film canisters to store beads, buttons, charms, and other small trinkets. If the container is opaque, glue a sample to the lid for easy identification.

3 You'll never need to hunt for or press trims again if you organize them on spools. Save empty cardboard tubes from paper towels, toilet tissue, or gift wrap. Wind on ribbon, rickrack, and other decorative trims. Secure the loose ends with straight pins or tape.

4 Some beads come pre-strung on single or multiple strands, called hanks. Keep the hanks in resealable clear plastic bags. Cut the string while it's inside the bag to access beads without worrying about spillage.

5 Plastic cases designed for storing children's toy cars and trucks are perfect for storing tall spools of decorative threads. They're two-sided, providing lots of storage, and clear, allowing you to identify the contents quickly. Because of their size and handle they're portable, too.

6 Check your local hardware or home improvement center for small, sturdy plastic storage units or cabinets. Many come equipped with multiple compartments or drawers designed for sorting nails, nuts, and bolts, but they're equally suitable for buttons, beads, jewels, sequins, or spools of thread.

7 Scour flea markets, garage sales, and church bazaars for vintage canning and storage jars, decorative tins, and old wooden cutlery caddies. Set these containers out where they will decorate your sewing space and provide easy access to tiny treasures. (Keep glass jars filled with embellishments away from direct sunlight.)

8 Your favorite fisherman can probably tell you about a system of interlocking, stacked plastic jars, used to separate and store fishing lures. These jars also make the perfect portable storage system for beads, sequins, and so forth. Look for these jars in sporting goods departments or stores that specialize in outdoor and fishing gear.

9 As libraries move into the computer age, card catalogs have become obsolete. These files are the perfect size for storing threads, rickracks, ribbons, pompoms, laces, and other larger embellishments. Check with your library. You just might walk away with a storage bargain!

10 A long, narrow bread basket, normally used for serving French bread, is perfect for storing carded ribbons, trims, flosses, and decorative threads. Sort the threads and trims by color, weight, or style, and stand the cards upright in the basket.

11 Organize embellishments for a work in progress with the help of a large, shallow basket. Get one that's already divided, or compartmentalize one with custard cups or other small containers. Use it to sort and store all the necessary embellishments, threads, needles, scissors, and other notions in one place.

12 For another simple work-in-progress solution, use a muffin tin or cupcake pan for sorting beads, buttons, jewels, sequins, studs, and other small, loose embellishments as you work.

13 While it's always a treat to discover vintage buttons at a flea market or tag sale, these aged treasures may require a little TLC before you can use them. Try a soft, lint-free cloth and a metal cleaner such as Brass-o to wipe down and reshine metallic buttons. (Test on the back first, to be sure the cleaner won't harm the finish.) Soak plastic, ivory, ceramic, or other similar buttons in a warm-water bath spiked with mild liquid detergent. If necessary, scrub gently with a soft vegetable brush or toothbrush. Rinse thoroughly, and dry with a soft towel.

14 To test the effects of light on the buttons, beads, and other embellishments you plan to use, place them on a sunny windowsill for about 2 weeks. This will indicate their potential for fading in direct sunlight.

15 Some glass beads lose their color when exposed to water—and you'll want to know *which* before sewing hundreds to a project you expect to launder. (Pink beads are known to be notorious offenders!) Place a sample of each bead you plan to use in a small bowl filled with warm water and liquid dish detergent. An hour-long soak will tell the tale.

16 Beading an item that will need to be dry-cleaned? Attach a bead to the cuff of a shirt or jacket that you're sending to the cleaner's first, to see how the bead stands up to the dry-cleaning chemicals.

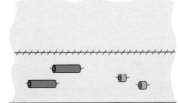

17 Don't automatically take an embellished project that needs dry cleaning to the same place where you take your shirts and suits. Choose a cleaner who specializes in caring for bridal or formalwear. He or she will already be familiar with the special requirements of beads, sequins, lace, and so on.

18 Gentle hand washing is highly recommended for any embellished item you need to launder. Prepare especially dense areas of embroidery, beading, or dimensional embellishment by basting voile or muslin over them. Turn garments inside out. Use cool water and a gentle soap formulated especially for textiles, such as Orvus or Vintage Textile Soak. Immerse the item in the cool, soapy bath, and allow it to soak (no scrubbing!). Rinse thoroughly, and lay flat to air dry.

19 Some buttons, such as precious antiques and those made from glass or china, should not be washed *or* dry-cleaned. Remove these buttons before laundering or cleaning and reattach them later.

20 Embellished wall pieces, with their various dimensional elements, get dusty. Occasional vacuuming is a safe, efficient way to keep them looking fresh. Either take the piece down or work right on the wall. To protect embellishments from breakage and suction, use a piece of fine mesh fiberglass screening (available at home improvement centers). Bind the edges with cloth or duct tape, hold the screening over the piece, and vacuum using the upholstery attachment.

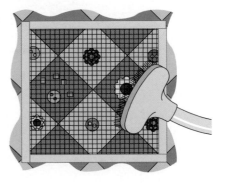

The 5 Ws
of Embellishment

*L*ike a star reporter covering the big story, a savvy embellisher needs to know the facts before stitching, stamping, or otherwise enhancing a quilting project. This chapter makes it easy. Here's where you'll find the classic 5 Ws: the who, what, where, when, and why of embellishing. This is headline news, so read this chapter first. Then read on for all the chapters that tell you the all-important "how!"

Getting Ready

This chapter is about thinking and observing; it's about discovering just what style and degree of ornamentation appeals to you and suits your needs. (Don't worry, there are plenty of hands-on techniques in the chapters to come!) As you decide which exciting technique to try first and you begin your collection of beads, buttons, threads, and trims, evaluate your personality, lifestyle, comfort zone, and time constraints. Do you make quilts and accessories for daily use, or garments reserved for special occasions? You may be a process person, who relishes the idea of lavishing hours on an intricate piece with thousands of beads and fine, delicate stitches. Or immediate gratification may be your goal, more likely to be met with quick, quirky rubber stamps or colorful splashes of fabric paint. Maybe you're somewhere in the middle. Do your tastes run to the timeless and traditional, spare and simple, baroque and bejeweled, or "red-hot and funky"? Whatever your needs or taste, you're bound to find inspiration and instructions to keep you embellishing for a long time to come.

Who

Special Considerations

Who will be using the finished quilt? Does the recipient's age, health, or lifestyle limit your embellishment options? **If the quilt is intended for an animal lover whose pets are allowed near or on the bed,** avoid dimensional or dangling doodads that might tempt an animal to chew. Skip buttons, beads, and charms on quilts for babies or toddlers, sticking to flat, easy-to-launder embellishments like stencils, rubber stamps, pintucks, or embroidery. **This quilt, featuring stamped floral images and free-motion machine quilting, is a safe choice for either situation.**

A Matter of Taste

Consider also the recipient's personality and taste, including their home or office decor. For example, **your best friend, who favors elegant, traditional interiors, might be most comfortable with a lushly embroidered and beribboned wall quilt in a subtle, neutral color scheme.** Your worldly daughter, on the other hand, might find a funky wall hanging, highly embellished with a dense assortment of innovative trims, the perfect accessory for her eclectic apartment. (See the piece shown at the bottom of this page.)

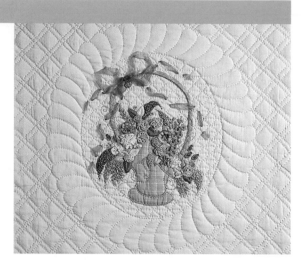

What

Tip

Determine whether the project's overall mood and design will be enhanced by embellishment before you start adding items to its surface.

Choose Your Candidate

What makes a good candidate for embellishment? In terms of the *type* of project, just about anything goes: wall hangings, bed quilts, pillows, quilted table accessories, and garments are just some of the possibilities. And it isn't just the arty project that benefits from a little dressing up. **Adorn your favorite traditional blocks or their contemporary cousins, such as this sunny Dresden Plate variation. Use elegant beads, theme-oriented buttons, yo-yos, or brightly colored rickrack, ribbons, and trims.**

Where

For Use or Display?

If you know where your project will be displayed, use that information to determine the choice and degree of embellishment. If the quilt is meant to be a bed covering, keep large, dimensional beads, buttons, charms, and other hard items to a minimum. Ditto for table runners, place mats, and other table coverings, where heavily dimensional embellishments can cause dishes or glassware to wobble. **Save more extroverted embellishments for strictly decorative items or art pieces, such as wall hangings.**

Effective Placement

The question of "where" also addresses where on the quilt, wall hanging, or garment you might place embellishment. Depending upon the effect you wish to create, where you'd like to focus attention, or what you might want to cover up, embellishment can be used to enhance individual appliqués and patches, blocks, sashes, borders, bindings, and other edging treatments.

When embellishing garments, think comfort. **Place larger buttons and beads mainly on the front.**

When

Timing Is Everything

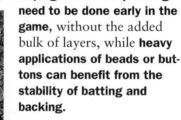

You'll need to determine exactly when in the construction process it's best to add embellishment. Base your decision on the particular technique and materials you plan to use. **For example, stamping and threadpainting need to be done early in the game,** without the added bulk of layers, while **heavy applications of beads or buttons can benefit from the stability of batting and backing.**

Tip

Particularly large, dimensional embellishments can interfere with quilting and might best be added when the quilting is complete.

Why

Just for the Fun of It

Why embellish? Perhaps the question should be "Why not?" Embellishment affords a wonderful opportunity to stretch your quilting repertoire with new techniques and materials and to flex your creative muscles. You can make a somewhat ordinary quilt into something extraordinary. But perhaps the best reason for embellishing is because it's fun! **Once you've invited beads, buttons, ribbons, rosettes, lamé, lace, and their friends into your sewing room, every project becomes a party!**

THE 5 WS OF EMBELLISHMENT

13

Put Couching
in Your Lineup

Couching may sound like a laid-back activity, but this technique for securing lines of decorative threads to fabric is simply jam-packed with exciting possibilities! You can accent design lines with subtlety or emphasize them big-time. The size and drama of the strand you couch determines the effect. So pull out those luscious threads, yarns, cords, braids, and trims you've been hoarding, and prepare to lay on the texture and sparkle!

Getting Ready

Prepare your sewing machine by changing to the appropriate foot, either an open-toe embroidery foot or a cording foot, depending on the thread or trim you plan to couch. (See the steps that follow for specific information.)

You can couch almost any thread you already have, and many quilt shops carry novelty threads designed especially for couching. But don't limit yourself to traditional choices. Look through your gift-wrapping, embroidery, knitting, crochet, and crafting supplies. Yarns—hefty or fine, lumpy or smooth, fuzzy wool or thick chenille—make wonderful couching materials, as do ribbons of every width, texture, and variety. Consider upholstery trim, metallic trim, lace, satin cord, or narrow strips of twisted or braided fabric. Even household twine and string assume new personality when couched to a quilt top.

The thread options for attaching decorative trims are as varied as the trims themselves. Stick with unobtrusive nylon monofilament, or add "splash" with variegated rayons or shimmering metallics.

What You'll Need

- **Quilt top**
- **Sketch for couching design**
- **Fabric marker**
- **Open-toe embroidery foot**
- **Cording foot (optional)**
- **Variety of threads for securing couching materials**
- **Tear-away stabilizer**
- **Variety of decorative threads to be couched**
- **Bobbinfil or lingerie thread**
- **Hand-sewing needle**
- **Seam sealant, such as FrayCheck (optional)**
- **Fabric scissors and thread snips**

Couching How-To

A wavy line that meanders from edge to edge across a quilt top makes an excellent choice for a couching novice. The gentle curve is easy to stitch, and the ends of both the decorative and stitching threads will be encased in a seam or covered by the binding, so you won't need to worry about them. Use a fabric marker such as a chalk pencil, water-soluble marker, or fine-lead mechanical pencil to **mark the couching design on your quilt top or block.** This marked line will eventually be covered with the couching thread, but you'll want it to remain visible as you stitch.

Tip

If you have difficulty seeing the line you have marked, stitch over it with a straight stitch before couching.

2

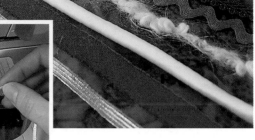

An open-toe embroidery foot works well for couching most decorative threads and trims. However, for couching round or slippery trims, a cording foot (sometimes called a braiding or piping foot) comes in handy. **This special attachment is grooved to accommodate the trim and often has a hole in front to feed the trim through.** You'll find it easier to "thread" the trim through the hole before attaching the foot to your sewing machine. Consult your machine manual for additional guidance.

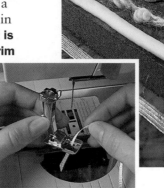

3

Select a thread to secure the decorative materials to your quilt. **To keep the securing stitching less noticeable and allow the trim to take center stage, choose an invisible monofilament thread or a thread that closely matches the trim in color or texture.** Use an appropriate machine needle for the securing thread.

Pin or baste a tear-away stabilizer to the back of your fabric wherever you plan to couch. This will prevent the "tunneling" (couching material sinking into the fabric) that a couching zigzag stitch often causes.

4

Fill the bobbin with lingerie, lightweight cotton, or bobbin thread such as Bobbinfil. Set your sewing machine to the zigzag stitch. Determine the correct stitch width by practicing with bits of your couching material on a large fabric scrap. (You may wish to practice with a contrasting-color couching thread, as shown here, so you can clearly gauge the results.) **Adjust the width of the zigzag stitch so that it is wide enough to just cover the trim, and be sure to keep the stitches centered over the trim as you sew.**

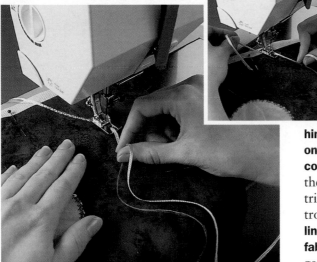

Bring the marked top to the sewing machine. Bring one end of the decorative trim through the hole in the foot, or center it under the machine foot at the beginning of a marked couching design. **Pull an 8-inch tail behind the presser foot. Hold the tail in one hand and begin stitching the couching material to the quilt.** Release the tail as the stitching secures the trim. Work slowly, to maintain control. **Position the trim over the marked line with one hand, and guide the fabric with the other.** After stitching, gently remove the tear-away stabilizer.

You'll need to finish off the ends of a couched line when it does not begin or end at an edge of the quilt. **Thread the trim and securing threads onto a hand-sewing needle, and bring them to the back of the fabric.** Use the stitching threads to secure the decorative thread with a knot or a backstitch. Trim all thread tails close to the fabric. Another option is to **leave the tails to hang freely as decorative elements.** Fray or knot the ends, or dab them with a sealant such as FrayCheck.

Tip

To finish off bulky threads and trims, thread them onto a tapestry, chenille, milliner's, or dollmaker's needle and bring them to the back of the work.

Variations

Couching Materials

After you've mastered the basics of couching, put your imagination into high gear. In addition to some of the more offbeat materials suggested in this chapter, use the basic zigzag stitch to attach rickrack, torn fabric strips (with raw edges exposed), silk cording, ribbon, chenille, and novelty yarns. **Make a stitching sampler, and note your favorites.** The more you experiment, the more likely it is that you won't settle for a merely good choice when there's the possibility of a fantastic one.

Tip

When stitching lots of dips and curves, narrow, flexible braids or cords and trims cut on the bias work best.

Stitching Threads

In addition to different decorative trims, experiment with a variety of stitching threads, as well. A stitching thread in an unexpected color can completely alter the look of the original trim. So can a thread of contrasting texture, such as a shiny rayon or glittery metallic.

Vary the Stitch

Once you're comfortable with the zigzag stitch for couching threads and trims, experiment with some of the other stitches hiding in your sewing machine. **Try substituting the feather stitch, blanket stitch, or even strings of cross-stitch stars, leaves, or vines to hold your decorative materials in place.**

Even a humble, straight line of stitching has a role to play. **Wide, flat trims or those with ruffled or lacy edges can be couched with straight or narrow satin stitches down the middle.**

Couching for Appliqués

Instead of using the usual satin stitch to finish the edges of fused appliqués, try couching. For best results, avoid motifs with lots of sharp points or tight curves.

Decide what effect you'd like to achieve (colors and textures that enhance or contrast with the appliqué), and choose trim and stitching threads accordingly. **Lay the trim so it just covers the raw edges of the appliqué, and couch with a zigzag** or other decorative stitch, as described in "Couching How-To" on page 15.

The Quilter's
Problem Solver

Couching as Quilting

Problem	Solution
You want to add couching to a quilt, but it's already layered and basted.	You can still add couching, even after your quilt has been sandwiched with batting and backing, and even if you've already quilted it. Since the stitches that secure the decorative trim penetrate all three quilt layers, they serve double-duty as quilting stitches, too. Work on a practice quilt sandwich until you feel comfortable. For hassle-free results, be sure your machine's upper tension is adjusted properly, and switch to a walking foot attachment. The latter feeds the layers evenly, which helps to avoid wrinkles and tucks, particularly on the quilt backing. Stitch slowly; you'll get the hang of it in no time!
You love the idea of couching and quilting in one step, but don't want all that zigzag stitching to show on the back of the quilt.	Minimize the appearance of stitching on the quilt back by matching the bobbin thread color to the backing fabric. Choose a multicolor, busy print for the backing; it makes better camouflage than a solid or a subtle tone-on-tone print.

Skill Builder

Turn corners with ease.

Occasionally you may need (or want) to turn a corner with your couching design. For a crisp, sharp corner, stop with the needle in the down position. If you arc turning the trim to the right, stop with the needle down to the right of the trim. If you are turning the trim to the left, stop with the needle down to the left of the trim. Raise the presser foot, pivot both the quilt and the trim, and continue, making sure the stitches remain centered over the trim.

Try This!

Use multiple threads and trims for added texture.

You needn't limit your couching material to a single strand of yarn, ribbon, or trim. Try mixing some of your favorites for totally different effects. Gather them loosely; twist, knot, or braid them; and then stitch them down with a straight or zigzag stitch.

Bring on *the Buttons!*

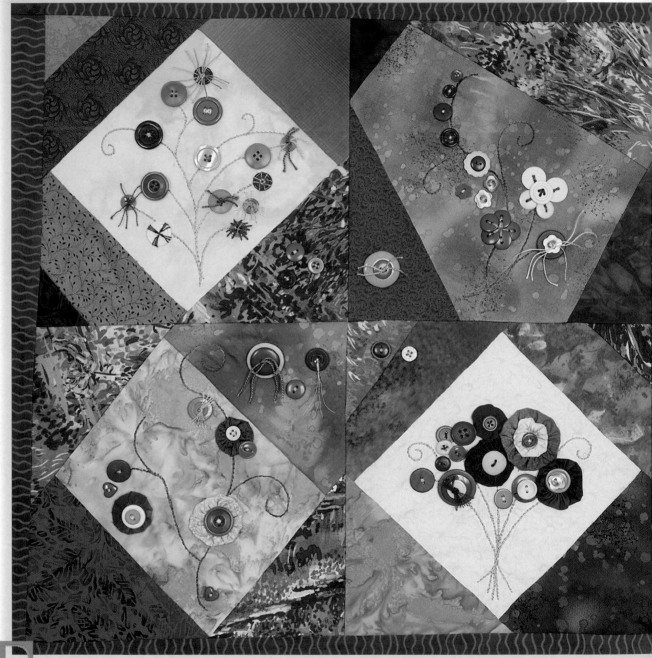

Even though it's often said in jest that "quilters don't do buttons" (on our husbands' shirts, anyway!), most of us will readily admit that these everyday embellishments have an undeniable appeal. For many of us, our first needle-and-thread experience involved the humble button. And who doesn't have happy memories of rummaging through Grandma's button box? There are buttons for every taste and pocketbook; purchase them by the scoopful for next to nothing, or splurge on antique or one-of-a-kind varieties. Either way, there's no doubt that buttons have a decorative appeal that far surpasses their functional applications.

Getting Ready

Different buttons create different effects, so choose your embellishments according to the mood or theme of your quilt. Plain Jane pearl or wooden buttons are homey and charming, with a definite folk art allure. Fancy metallic, porcelain, and glass buttons can be elegant and refined—the "glamour girls" of the button world.

You'll want to have extra-sturdy thread on hand to sew these treasures to your quilts. Strong, all-purpose cotton thread, quilting thread, button and carpet thread, and even nylon beading thread (such as Nymo or Silamide) are all good choices.

Most frequently, you'll want to stitch buttons to a layered, if not quilted, surface. If you need to work on a quilt top, do as shirt-makers do: Place a small circle of interfacing or felt behind the fabric, and stitch the button through this extra layer as well.

In any case, we can't say it enough: For safety's sake, don't put buttons on quilts for babies and young children.

The Scoop on Buttons

Basic Button Types

There are two main varieties of buttons: those with sew-through holes (usually two or four) and those with a loop or shank on the back for attaching them. You can use either type to embellish your quilts. Stitches are visible to varying degrees for sew-through buttons, depending on the method and materials you select. Stitches attaching shank buttons are usually not visible. Another factor to consider: Sew-throughs usually lie flat on the surface, while buttons with shanks often sit above the quilt surface.

Attaching Sew-Through Buttons

Tip

For extra pizzazz, string seed beads onto the thread as you're sewing across the holes of a button.

There are countless ways to sew on a sew-through button! You may be used to the standard cross stitch over four holes, using matching sewing thread, but consider other patterns, decorative threads or embroidery floss, and accent colors. Connect four holes in pairs for parallel rows of stitching, and then add perpendicular rows to form a square. Work thread over the edges of the button. Hide the securing knots beneath the button or between the layers of the quilt, or tie them off on top of the buttons. Leave these thread ends to dangle or fan out.

Stack 'Em Up

Tip

Use velvets and silks to create a crazy-pieced background for a grouping of elegant metallic and glass buttons.

For added interest, group buttons together in clusters (odd numbers often look best). **Take this idea even further, and stack buttons on top of one another, either directly or in staggered arrangements.** As you do this, be creative with your attaching stitches, perhaps bringing the thread over the edges of the buttons, or tying and fringing the thread on top.

You can also use buttons to attach, and further enhance, other embellishments. For example, tack down yo-yo flowers with large button centers.

Attaching Shank Buttons

Tip

Thread color isn't critical, because the button will cover the stitches, but a matching or neutral shade is always a safe choice.

Use a strong, double strand of sewing or quilting thread to attach shank-style buttons to a quilt top, catching the batting in your stitches (and the backing as well, if you want the button to sink into the surface).

If you want a shank button to lay flat against the surface of the quilt, you can **use pliers to twist off metal shanks or break off plastic shanks.** Then glue the button in place with strong glue.

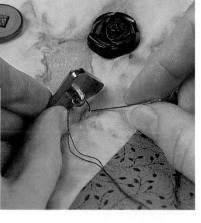

Even the simplest buttons can add texture and detail to your quilt designs—detail that is difficult to achieve with appliqué. **Tiny buttons provide the ideal substitute for time-consuming, circular appliqués, such as the eye on a bird, or berries paired with leaves.** You might also decorate a pieced or appliquéd holiday tree with brightly colored button ornaments, or send a train down the track on round button wheels of various sizes.

Theme Enhancers

Novelty buttons add never-fail visual appeal to pictorial quilts. Include these whimsical embellishments, available in thousands of different shapes and sizes, to advance your quilt's "story" and further enhance its theme. In this example, **the clever use of cracker-shaped buttons heightens the visual humor of "Tea at the Ritz."**

Tip

While you're checking out theme fabrics and conversation prints at your local fabric store, take a look at the latest novelty buttons.

Adding Whimsy

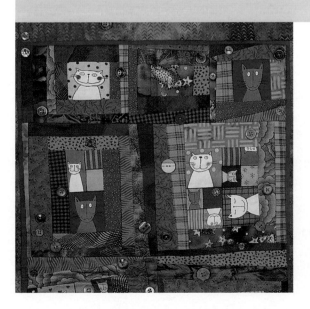

Punctuate a humorous, folk art, or scrappy quilt with a random sprinkling of old, unmatched buttons. Look for jars and tins of these buttons in grandma's attic, at antique shows, and at estate, garage, or tag sales.

Attach buttons of various sizes and colors after you've machine quilted your project. Short on time? **Simply tie, or "tuft," the quilt with buttons,** as on this patchwork runner. Using a double strand of sewing thread and a large-eye needle, come up from the back, sew through a button, and return the needle to the back. Knot the thread ends and trim them short.

Tip

Hand wash old buttons, or any project that features them, using cool water and a gentle soap.

BRING ON THE BUTTONS!

Buttons Undercover

It's easy and fun to make your own custom buttons to perfectly complement your quilt. Visit the notions department of a fabric store and purchase cover-your-own button kits, used by dressmakers to make matching fabric-covered buttons for garments. **Use the accent fabrics in your quilt to cover these nifty button foundations,** following the manufacturer's instructions.

Thinking Outside the Box

Tip

Draw faces on smooth-surfaced, shank-type buttons using fine-tip permanent markers. Embroider or appliqué the bodies.

You needn't limit yourself to literal interpretations when choosing buttons to embellish your quilts. Focus on buttons of similar shape or configuration, or those that merely suggest the image you wish to convey. **For example, pencil-shape buttons become playful legs for the figures on a whimsical quilt** by Rachel Roggel, shown here and below.

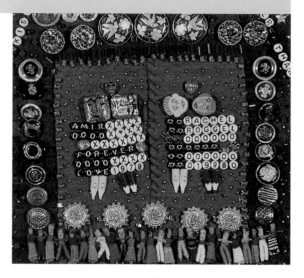

Go Crazy with Buttons!

Why not make the buttons themselves the stars of your quilt? Compose an art quilt using buttons as you would dabs of paint on a canvas. Play different textures, colors, and materials against each other. **You may even wish to encrust entire sections of the quilt with dozens of buttons.** For this treatment, you may want to fuse a layer of interfacing to the wrong side of the quilt top for stability. And use a dense, stable batting **so your finished work of art hangs nice and straight.**

The Quilter's
Problem Solver

Keeping Buttons in Their Place

Problem	Solution
You're sewing *lots* of buttons on a quilt you plan to exhibit, and you want to make sure they stay securely attached through packing, shipping, and display.	❑ Starting with a sturdy cotton, quilting, or nylon beading thread will definitely help. A new spool is best, as thread left to languish on the shelf becomes dry and brittle due to age, heat, and light. ❑ Even if you're attaching many buttons in a close area, tie off frequently. Make a knot after every three or four buttons before continuing. That way, if the thread should wear and break at some point, you won't lose all of your handiwork! ❑ If you're *still* concerned that a thread might not be sturdy enough, put a tiny dot of glue on the back of each button before stitching it to the quilt.

Skill Builder

Use buttonholes as embellishments, too.

With its strong, linear shape, the buttonhole can make a splendid embellishment on its own. Refer to your sewing machine manual for details concerning setup, foot attachment, and corded buttonhole options. Practice until you are able to get neat, attractive results. Experiment with varying lengths and widths, random and repeating arrangements, individual units and clusters. Try them in contrasting cotton or glossy decorative threads. Once you've explored the options, stitch them on your quilt blocks, in sashes, or on borders, for a unique visual and textural accent. You can leave them uncut if you wish, or cut them open for an unexpected, arty touch.

Try This!

Make buttons from polymer compound.

For the ultimate in designer buttons, make your own with an oven-baked clay. One versatile material sold under brand names such as Sculpey or Fimo comes in cakes of various colors and also in handy, easy-to-use rolls that are already shot through with pattern and color. Slice the exact number of buttons you want, in whatever thickness you desire. Use a toothpick to pierce holes for sew-through buttons, or insert an eye ring to make a shank. Then bake the buttons according to the manufacturer's directions.

BRING ON THE BUTTONS!

The Basics
of Beading

Quilters have been sewing beads onto quilts since crazy quilts became the rage in the latter half of the 19th century. Nowadays, you needn't make one particular style of quilt to experience the pleasures of beading. Beads made from glass, metal, ceramics, wood, semi-precious stones, and countless other natural and synthetic materials might enliven traditional blocks, emphasize key design elements, secure buttons and charms, or infuse your quilt with overall sparkle and rich surface texture. Our step-by-step instructions for hand and machine beading lay the foundation for a myriad of creative options.

Getting Ready

Of the hundreds of types of beads, the seed bead is the smallest and perhaps most versatile, with the thin, cylindrical bugle bead a close second. We focus on these two basic bead families, but you can adapt the same techniques to any small beads, including the specialty beads described on page 33.

You can purchase beads mixed or matched, loose in a tube, by the "threaded" strand, in multiple strands called hanks, and even by the individual bead for some unique, unusual varieties. Visit local quilt, needlework, or craft shops for beads and basic beading supplies. Investigate bead vendors at large quilt shows, and check Internet and mail-order resources.

Work on an uncluttered, flat surface. A shallow dish will corral loose beads and let you insert the tip of a needle through a bead without picking up the bead in your hand. Or, place beads on a 6-inch scrap of felt or Ultrasuede. The nap of the fabric grips the beads so they don't roll around. Use a light-color scrap for dark beads, and vice versa.

What You'll Need

Layered quilt sandwich

Variety of seed, bugle, and other beads

Embroidery scissors or thread snips

Removable fabric marker

Variety of hand-sewing needles

Strong, fine thread such as Nymo or Silamide

Sewing machine

Sewing machine needles in various sizes

Fine, strong thread for machine needle and bobbin

Beading bobbin (nylon monofilament wound on cardboard bobbin)

Tweezers

Hand Beading

Needles & Threads

There are many types of needles and threads available for beading. The best beading techniques require stitching through beads two or more times, so select a needle with the largest possible eye that will still pass through a previously strung bead. Beading needles are long and fine, but sometimes are not strong enough to go through very heavy fabrics. You can try fine appliqué, size 9 embroidery, or size 10 quilting needles (betweens). Your thread should match or blend with the color of your beads. Nymo and Silamide are two brands especially intended for beadwork.

When choosing a needle size, note that the numbers on all sewing and beading needles correspond to the sizes of seed beads.

THE BASICS OF BEADING

Starting Off

Tip

You can carefully hand quilt after beading, but always machine quilt *before* adding beads.

Start with a sample quilt sandwich or a small quilted project. Thread your needle with a 15- to 18-inch length of thread. Knot the end of the thread and insert the needle into the top and batting about 1 inch away from where the bead will be. Bring the needle up just to the left of the spot where you wish to position the first bead. **Give the thread a tug to bury the knot in the batting, just as you would for hand quilting.** Note: Here, as in the rest of the hand-beading instructions, reverse directions if you are left-handed.

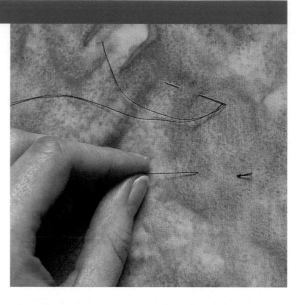

The Basic Backstitch

Tip

Bead and quilt at the same time by adding a bead on a backstitch every few quilting stitches.

The backstitch is a durable way to attach beads. Pick up the first bead with the tip of the threaded needle. **Reinsert the needle one bead-width to the right of where the needle first emerged, and back out where the thread first emerged.** Pass the needle under the quilt top to make the bead "float" on top, or through the batting to make it sink into the layers. Pass the needle back through the bead, **into the fabric (and batting, if desired), then over to a spot just to the left of where you want to place the next bead.**

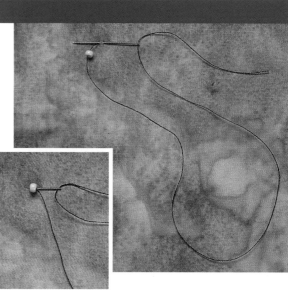

Scatter-Stitch Beading

Tip

If you wish to distance your beads more than a needle's length apart, use a thimble to help you navigate the needle through the batting.

Pull the thread snug so the bead lies flat on the surface of the quilt, but not so tight that the fabric puckers. The bead should stand up like a car tire. **For a random application of beads, add them one at a time as indicated above.** Travel between the quilt layers with the threaded needle, then bring it up just to the left of where you want the next bead to go. To tie off your thread, make a tiny backstitch that will be hidden under the last bead. Pass the threaded needle through the batting to bury the tail, and clip the thread where it reemerges.

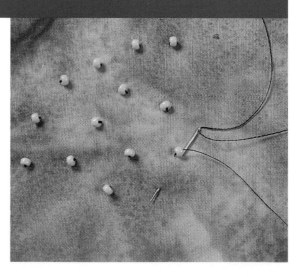

Continuous-Line Beading

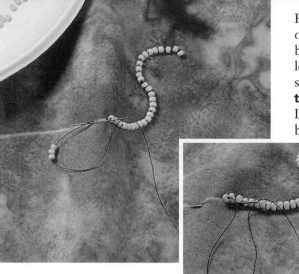

For a curved line, add beads one by one as previously indicated, placing beads at close intervals, and following the line with your back-stitches. **For a straight line, string up to three small beads on the needle.** Insert the needle into the fabric and bring it up where the thread emerged previously. Next, pass the needle back through the beads and into the fabric. Make a *third* pass through only the last bead on the row, **then travel three bead-widths further along the line to continue.**

Tip

To bead a continuous line, lightly mark the design line with a fabric marker.

Attaching Bugle Beads

Bugle beads are thin, tubular beads available in a variety of colors and lengths (usually ⅛ inch to 2 inches long). The cut ends are sharp, so it's even more important than for seed beads that you backstitch them on securely, passing the thread through two or even three times. **Allow one full bead-length when bringing the threaded needle up to add each new bead.** More than that, and the bugle saws back and forth and breaks the thread; less than that, and you'll have puckers in the fabric.

Tip

When it comes to size, the larger the number, the larger the bugle bead. The exact opposite is true for seed beads.

Bugle Bead Variations

Bugle beads can be sewn end to end in a long row, side by side to form a "fence," or scattered randomly at varying distances and angles to add allover sparkle. You can also mix seed beads and bugle beads. They team up very effectively to provide visual variety and additional design possibilities. For example, **you can use seed beads as spacers between bugle beads to achieve smoothly curved lines and spirals.**

Tip

Give new life to old beads: Check yard sales and thrift shops for jewelry that can be disassembled.

THE BASICS OF BEADING

Bugle Beads for Impact

Because of their size, bugle beads reflect more light and therefore sparkle more than seed beads. Notice the small quilt on page 26; even nestled in a tangle of colorful threads, the bugle beads are very effective accents. And, because of their shape, bugle beads are great for creating or reinforcing directional design elements. **A leaf motif on a quilt gets a well-defined vein as well as a lot of pizzazz with copper-color bugle beads.**

Beaded Appliqués

Tip

Consider using interestingly shaped beads, such as little glass leaves with wire loops, from Mill Hill.

Try using beads and the basic backstitch for tacking ribbon, ruched or silk flowers, leaves, stems, or other dimensional appliqués to your quilts. Select the type, style, color, or size bead that will give you the effect you're looking for. These dimensional flowers are attached with larger beads, sometimes called pebble or pony beads, $3/16$ inch in size. Allow romantic satin or silk ribbon to undulate over the surface of your quilt, securing it here and there or at regular intervals with seed beads of complementary or contrasting colors.

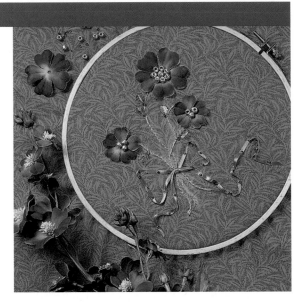

Dangling Beads

Tip

See "Taking Trims to the Edge" on page 110 for beaded fringe.

Let hanging beads add excitement to your wall hangings. **Attach short fringes of beads in varying types, sizes, colors, and shapes.** Select a long needle and thread it with a strong, neutral-color nylon thread, securing the thread with a buried knot. String beads on the thread, mixing colors, shapes, and sizes of beads to get the most interesting effect. Add a small bead to cover the hole of the last bead on the strand or make a double or triple knot. Then bring the needle and thread back up through the row of beads. Make a backstitch at the top of the dangling row.

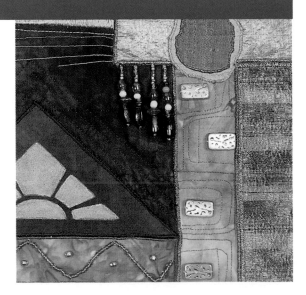

Machine Beading

Machine beading is really just couching with strings of beads. **Use a needle to string beads onto strong monofilament thread on a beading bobbin** (actually just a small spool).

Some beads come strung on cotton thread, but this thread is not reliably strong. You can replace it easily, though: Clip the knot at one end, then tie this end of the cotton thread to the end of the monofilament, making a small, neat knot. **Slide the beads off the cotton thread and onto the monofilament.**

Tip

If an occasional bead won't slide over the knot, don't force it. Break it with pliers and discard it.

Practice on a sample quilt sandwich or work on a quilt top that has been reinforced with a fusible or tear-away stabilizer. Use a fine, strong thread, such as lingerie nylon, on top and in the bobbin. For beads too large to fit under a cording foot, remove the presser foot, drop or cover the feed dogs, and lower the take-up lever. Insert the threaded needle at the desired location of the first bead. Holding the tail of the top thread, hand-turn the balance wheel to draw up the bobbin thread. **Tie the needle thread to the beading bobbin thread with a tiny, secure knot.**

Tip

To secure a string of consistently small beads, a cording foot with a groove will give you an easier time and greater control.

Set the machine to sew a narrow zigzag stitch. Place the beading bobbin and all but one bead to the left of the needle so they are handy, but out of the way as you work. Pull the knotted end of the monofilament and the single bead around in front of the needle, close to the eye. Hold the top and bottom threads firmly in one hand, and sew three or four tiny zigzag stitches in one place over the monofilament to secure it. **Using tweezers, push the bead right up to the stitching.**

Tip

If you wish to machine bead a very precise line or shape, mark the desired pattern with a removable fabric marker.

THE BASICS OF BEADING

4

Tip

A cool option: Use a decorative thread in the needle, and sew a narrow satin stitch over the thread between each bead.

Turning the balance wheel manually or working very slowly, take about three zigzag stitches right in front of the first bead, over the monofilament thread. **Use tweezers to move a new bead into position,** and then zigzag in front of it in the same way.

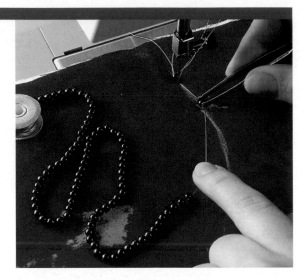

5

Continue adding beads in this manner until the beaded row is complete. Leave the needle up to position beads close together; leave it down if you prefer to keep the quilt sandwich secure. Place your stitches along the marked line, and keep the spacing and number of zigzag stitches between beads consistent. To end a row of beading, cut the monofilament, leaving an 8-inch tail. Bring this tail back under the last few beads, and zigzag stitch a couple of times between each of the last four beads. Use a hand needle to bury all thread tails.

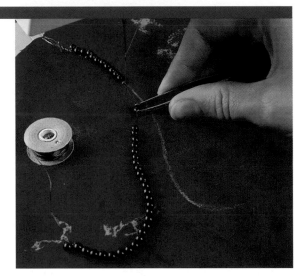

Showcasing Single Beads

Tip

With this technique, consider a decorative top thread, such as a rayon or metallic.

To attach loose beads by machine, use a needle fine enough to fit through the hole in the bead. Work without any foot attachment and with the feed dogs dropped or covered, **free-motion stitching between beads in any pattern you wish.** Make a few tiny free-motion stitches to start and end a line of stitches, and before and after each bead. Use tweezers to position a bead hole-side-up on the fabric, and hand turn the balance wheel to lower the needle into the bead. Take a single stitch to secure the bead. **Short curving lines of stitches with a bead secured at the center give you a whimsical look.**

32

The Quilter's
Problem Solver

Exploring Bead Options

Problem

You want to add beading to your next project, but you don't want to restrict yourself to bugle and seed beads.

Solution

There are many different types of beads, and most come in a wide variety of colors and sizes.

❑ *Transparent.* You can see through this finish, whether the beads are clear or colored.

❑ *Color-lined.* Transparent beads that feature holes lined in a contrasting color.

❑ *Metallic-lined.* Transparent beads that feature a silver, gold, or other metallic hole lining.

❑ *Rocailles* is a term used in the U.S. to denote seed beads with square holes, usually silver-lined.

❑ *Charlottes* are manufactured in the Czech Republic and are made from seed beads. They have one facet ground into them, hence the alternate names *One-cut* or *true-cut.*

❑ *3-cuts* are also Czech-made beads. They are made from canes of six-sided glass, using a manufacturing process that takes three hand-controlled passes through the grinding machine.

❑ *Cylinder beads* are Japanese-made glass beads with thin walls, polished ends, and a large hole for easy threading. You may find them identified by the trade names Delicas or Antiques.

❑ *Triangles* are made in Japan and feature three rounded edges. They're made of glass and come in three sizes.

❑ *Square* and *hex* beads are shaped as their names imply. Square beads are Japanese-made and come in one size only (4 mm). Hex beads are made from a cane of six-sided glass and are also known as 2-Cuts.

Rocailles   **Triangle**   **Square**   **Hex**

Opt for a hoop.

While a hoop is not necessary for hand beading, you may feel more comfortable working in a hoop if you normally use one for hand quilting. If you choose this option, keep the tension in the hoop loose enough to maneuver the threaded needle easily between the layers of the quilt sandwich. In addition, plan your beading strategy in advance, as you won't want to reposition the hoop over a previously beaded area and risk damaging the beads.

Try This!

Make the thread part of the embellishment.

To attach individual beads dramatically, use a decorative strand of colorful rayon or shiny metallic thread, or consider ⅛-inch satin or silk ribbon. Bring the threaded needle through the bead, and then sew long and short straight stitches radiating outward from the bead on one side, opposite sides, or outward all around.

Spread Your Wings
with Hand Embroidery

Maybe you've inherited a packet of vintage redwork patterns ideal for transformation into a family heirloom quilt. Or perhaps your newly completed appliqué block or pieced colorwash design cries out for added dimension and detail. If you wonder where to start, a quick glance through the next few pages is sure to give your imagination wings. You'll be bursting to try your hand at embroidery, the common thread that can bring any project to life.

Getting Ready

Hand embroidery provides an almost inexhaustible source of embellishment possibilities, with an endless mix of stitches, threads, and techniques. Linear stitches, such as the stem stitch or the chain stitch, define shapes and add lines of detail to your quilt designs. When worked densely over an area, these stitches can fill in a shape and provide subtle texture. For more drama, try dimensional stitches (those that stand away from the surface), such as the French knot or turkey work. Refer to "Embroidery Stitch Details" on page 41.

A comfortable chair and footstool will enhance your stitching experience. So will adequate lighting. A shallow embroidery hoop, 5 to 14 inches in diameter, will help keep your stitches smooth and consistent. (Determine hoop size by the dimensions of the embroidered piece.) For added stability, you may wish to back small pieces, such as small wall hangings or decorative pillows, with thin cotton or lightweight fusible interfacing prior to stitching.

What You'll Need

Block, quilt, or garment ready for embroidery

Embroidery pattern

Pencil

Light box

Variety of threads, flosses, and ribbons

Paper towel

Glass bowl

Vinegar and measuring cup

Variety of needles in various sizes

Embroidery hoops in various sizes

Embroidery and fabric scissors

Iron and pressing surface

Polyester batting or polyester fiberfill (optional)

Embroidery Essentials

Choosing a Technique

For the best results, select a project or pattern with techniques suited to your level of stitching experience. For example, a beginner might be comfortable trying traditional redwork. This embroidery form, which has recently enjoyed a renaissance among quiltmakers, eliminates sometimes-confusing decisions about what colors to use; the stitcher is free to concentrate on learning the stitches. Begin with the basic stem stitch to outline a design. Once you become more advanced, you can **incorporate a variety of lavish embellishing stitches with dimensional effects.**

Transferring Patterns

Tip

Elegant, traditional wallpaper motifs, such as large paisleys and florals, make wonderful sources for embroidery designs.

Embroidery patterns can be found in needlework books and magazines and at fabric, needlework, and quilt shops. You can also design your own patterns freehand or by using the line drawings in a child's coloring book or your favorite appliqué designs as a starting point. Cut a slightly oversize piece of background fabric. (You can trim and square the block later.) Tape the pattern on a light box, if you have one. Tape the fabric over the pattern, and **use a lead pencil to *lightly* trace the pattern onto the background fabric.** The embroidery will cover the pencil marks.

Selecting Threads

Tip

When choosing pearl cotton, remember: the lower the thread number, the finer the thread.

The mood of the piece you are making helps determine which threads will be most appropriate. **Make a sampler of threads, and compare their textures.** Cotton floss is best for traditional redwork because it is easy to work with and reliably colorfast. Heavier pearl cotton #5 is great for covering large areas quickly. Silk or fine rayons are smooth and glossy, wonderful for working an elegant satin stitch. For a folk art look, try threads that are darker in color, have a matte finish, or are of a coarser texture, such as crewel wool.

Needle Know-How

Choose a needle based upon the thread you plan to use. A sharp crewel or embroidery needle, with its long, oval eye, is a good choice for flosses and some metallics. A darning needle is a strong, large-eyed needle that works well with bulkier threads and fibers, such as wool and pearl cotton. The small, round eye of the milliner's needle makes it ideal for finer silks, metallics, and single-filament threads, while the sharp, oval-eyed chenille needle is a natural for silk ribbon work.

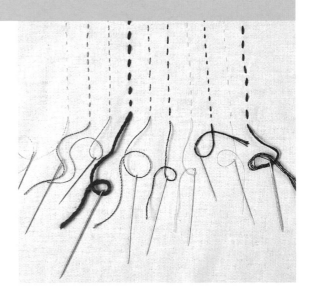

Mixing Threads

For delightful special effects, thread your needle with strands of thread in different colors or values (and even fibers). It's easy to separate individual strands of six-strand embroidery floss and recombine them. In the sample at left, each line of chain stitches ending in a tassel uses four strands of floss. **From left to right, the mixes consist of: four strands of red; three strands of red and one of dark red; three strands of red and one of pink; two strands of red, one each of rose and pink; and one strand each of red, dark red, rose, and pink.**

Tip

Use Tiger Tape to keep straight lines of embroidery stitches even and consistent.

Testing for Colorfastness

When choosing threads, colorfastness is of the utmost importance. While most manufacturers state the colorfastness of their products on the thread label, you'll need to test any unmarked threads you buy or find in your stash. Wet a paper towel or white cloth with very warm water, place the skein in the cloth, and squeeze it gently. **If color appears, the thread is not colorfast.** Use a bath of 1 part vinegar to 4 parts water to set the color. Rinse well in cool water, and dry flat. If color residue appears after two treatments, do not use that particular thread.

Starts & Stops

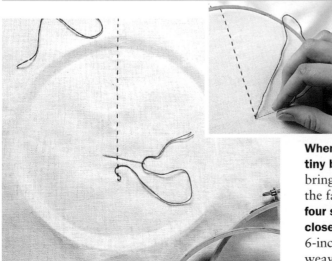

Knots can cause unsightly lumps on the front of finished work. To eliminate this problem, work with an unknotted thread. Begin your stitching, leaving a 6-inch thread tail on the wrong side of your work. **When you've finished stitching, take a tiny backstitch under the last stitch,** bring the needle to the wrong side of the fabric, **weave it through two to four stitches, and clip the thread close to the surface.** Rethread the 6-inch tail, take a tiny backstitch, and weave and clip it in the same way.

Tip

If you're using heavy, multiple strands, reduce bulk by trimming one tail end after it's been woven under two stitches, another after three stitches, and so on.

SPREAD YOUR WINGS WITH HAND EMBROIDERY

Pressing Embroidery

The embroidered piece will get lots of handling as you work on it and will likely become wrinkled from the hoop, so you'll probably want to gently wash and press it. Use cool water and a gentle soap, and let it dry slightly. Then select an iron setting appropriate for the most delicate thread used, and **press the finished piece from the back.** When you've finished pressing, turn the piece over to the front, and use your fingers to fluff dimensional details back into shape.

Linear Stitches at Work

Outlining Appliqués

To focus attention on an appliqué shape, stitch around the motif (just inside the edge or perhaps along it) with a linear stitch such as the chain stitch. **This embroidery can also be used to simultaneously appliqué a turned or raw-edge shape in place.** Choose a matching thread color for a subtle effect or a thread of lighter or darker value for more notice. Embellish the stitch and the motif further **by adding a whip or weaving stitch as well, such as these leaf veins worked in the woven running stitch.**

Alternative Outliners

In addition to the usual stem, outline, chain, and running stitches, a number of other stitches work well for attaching, outlining, and enhancing appliqués. **Any of the blanket stitch variations add pleasing detail and texture.** Choose your thread based upon the look and mood of the overall piece. For an elegant mood, use shiny rayons or metallics; for homespun flavor, use pearl cotton or floss. Since these stitches "bite" into the appliqué, they are great for securing the edges of fused appliqués.

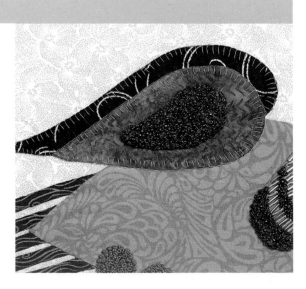

Providing Detail

Linear embroidery stitches can add literal detail to appliqué designs. In this block, chain stitches delineate the curving neck of a bird—a difficult feat to accomplish with only a cut piece of fabric. Chain-stitched curlicues extend the tail-feather appliqués into the background in slender, gracefully curved lines.

Think about using embroidery to embellish your patchwork as well: Work stem stitches in coarse thread to add woven-look texture to a pieced basket, or use silk thread to create striations in the petals of a Carolina Lily block.

Adding Texture

If luxurious, textured stitchery suits your fancy, try combining two or more embroidery stitches. In this block, the leaves and flowers were appliquéd in a traditional fashion. Gold metallic embroidery thread is used to work a grid of long, straight stitches in each of the small oval leaves. The large magnolia buds feature a stem-stitched grid with a tiny gold cross-stitch at each intersection, and a French knot inside each square of the grid. For maximum impact, use different colors or textures of thread for each different stitch.

Tip

Use neutral or softly muted threads and a combination of embroidery stitches to tone down overly bright or too-obvious appliqués.

Linear Stitches Fill In

By placing linear stitches in dense rows, you can fill an area with color and texture. Long, straight stitches side by side make up the well-known satin stitch. **But for a different texture, consider the chain stitch, as shown on this bird's crest and tail feathers.** Such an embroidery treatment takes the place of appliqué, creating filled-in areas of any size and shape you require.

Dimensional Stitches

Dimensional stitches, such as French knots, turkey work, bullion stitch, and spiderweb stitch, add interest to any embroidered, pieced, or appliquéd design. Use them individually as eyes for animals, scatter them on vines or stems as seeds or berries, or group them to add realistic detail to flower centers. **Clustered tightly together, these stitches can add loads of textural impact, as in the turkey work bird's head, bullion stitch mop-top crest, and spiderweb flower heads.**

Appliquéd Embroidery

Tip

Fill in the edge with additional stitches if necessary to hide the turned-under seam.

Clustered embroidery techniques can put undue stress on the embellished fabric. To minimize this stress, trace the shape for the dense treatment onto another fabric, place it in a hoop, and embroider it separately. **Begin at the outside and work toward the center.** Cut out the finished embroidery, **adding a small seam allowance all around.** Pin the appliqué to the background, placing the pins near the edges of the shape and pointing them inward. Appliqué the embroidery to your project with matching thread.

Padded Embroidery

Tip

You can also use trapunto to add dimension. Complete the appliqué work, slit the background from the back, insert stuffing, and whipstitch the slit closed.

To give appliquéd embroidery more dimension, consider padding it for an elegant raised effect. For a ball shape, you can run gathering stitches around a small circular piece, just as for a yo-yo, and **stuff it with a bit of polyester fiberfill or a scrap of polyester batting** before pulling the stitches taut to close. Then, **simply appliqué the embroidered shape to the background.** For other shapes, begin appliquéing the embroidered piece around the edges, and insert a filler material before completing the appliqué stitching.

Embroidery Stitch Details

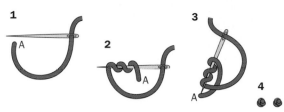

Backstitch

Blanket Stitch

French Knot

(1) Bring the threaded needle up at A. (2) Holding the thread taut, wrap it around the needle 3 times. (3) Insert the tip of the needle back into the fabric, close to A. Pull the needle down through the fabric, holding the thread taut until thread is pulled through the wraps of thread, forming a knot (4).

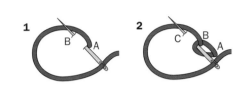

Chain Stitch

Satin Stitch

Running Stitch   Whipped Running Stitch

Turkey Work

Make evenly staggered, overlapping backstitches, pulling odd stitches tightly, and leaving even stitches loose to form loops. For a fuzzy effect, make a series of close rows to form a pile, and clip the loops, trimming them to the same height.

Cross Stitch   Stem Stitch

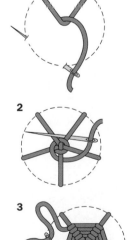

Spiderweb Stitch

(1) Lay the spokes of the web, making sure you have an odd number. Bring the needle up at the center and (2) begin weaving under and over spokes, keeping the thread on top of the fabric. (3) For a different, more dimensional effect, do not weave; instead, use the needle to wrap the thread around each spoke as you come to it.

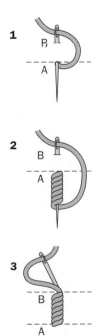

Bullion Stitch

(1) Bring the needle up through the fabric at A, down at B, and up at A again; do not pull the needle through. (2) Wrap the thread around the needle point 5 to 7 times as needed to cover the A to B distance. Carefully pull the needle through both fabric and wraps. (3) Pull wraps toward point B so the coil can lay flat. Pull the core thread tight and use the point of the needle to pack wraps together evenly. Reinsert the needle into point B.

Magical
Machine Embroidery

Y ou may not know it, but your sewing machine conceals a treasure chest of decorative stitchery! It needn't be a fancy machine, with computer hook-up or preprogrammed embroidery cards. A reliable model that's capable of an assortment of basic stitches, such as the zigzag, blanket, and feather stitch, can produce fantastic results. This chapter gives you the keys—and the confidence—to master and go beyond these basic stitches to unlock the wonders of machine embroidery. The results? Quilts rich in added texture and color… the kind you just can't help but touch.

Getting Ready

One of the most intriguing features of machine embroidery is its unlimited potential; you'll want to explore all the options. This chapter will guide you through a series of sample swatches. Before long, you'll be using the various techniques to create custom fabric or to add texture and detail to blocks, sashes, borders, or even your completed quilt top.

Be sure your machine is clean, oiled, and in good condition, and make sure you have the manual handy. Get a comfortable chair and a good sewing lamp. Machine embroidery is addictive: You'll probably be at it for a while!

A variety of decorative threads, flat ribbons, and narrow cords will increase your creative options. Functional threads such as mercerized cotton, dressmaker's polyester, lingerie nylon, Bobbinfil, and Metrolene will be useful, as well.

Choose solid or quiet print fabrics for your machine-embroidered projects so that the decorative stitches will be clearly visible. A tight, firm weave is optimal, such as the medium-weight linen used throughout this chapter.

What You'll Need

Solid color or tone-on-tone medium-weight fabric

Lightweight iron-on fusible or tear-away stabilizer

Rotary-cutting equipment

Straight pins

Fabric marking pencils

Variety of functional and decorative sewing threads

Variety of presser feet (embroidery, open-toe, and darning)

Variety of sewing machine needles, such as embroidery (75/90), topstitch (100), and double needle (2.0 or 3.0)

Fabric and embroidery scissors

Sewing machine capable of basic decorative stitches

Sewing machine manual

Decorative Stitching Basics

Use a fusible interfacing or a tear-away stabilizer on the wrong side of the fabric so the stitches won't "sink in" or cause puckering as you sew. If you are using fusible interfacing, bond it to your fabric and cut the fabric into 6-inch squares for practice swatches. If you are using a tear-away stabilizer, cut both the fabric and stabilizer into 6-inch squares and pin them together. **With a fabric pencil, draw simple designs on a few of the reinforced fabric squares.**

1

2

Thread your sewing machine with a decorative thread such as rayon or embroidery cotton and fill the bobbin with a lightweight all-purpose thread such as Metrolene or lingerie thread. **Refer to your machine and its manual to choose a decorative stitch** and determine the appropriate stitch settings (length and width). Loosen the top tension (lower the number) by a half-increment so the decorative thread sews fuller on top. An open-toe foot will accommodate most decorative stitches.

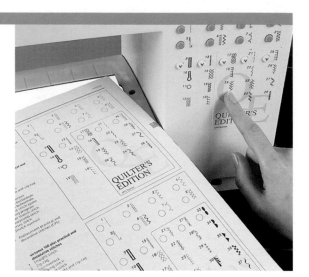

Tip

If, despite reinforcement, your fabric buckles or puckers when stitched, switch to a heavier-weight fusible or stabilizer.

3

Draw the bobbin thread up, pull both the top and bobbin threads behind the presser foot, and insert the needle at the beginning of the design you've marked on your practice square. Set the stitch width and length to 0 and take a few stitches in place. (On a computerized machine, you can use the lock stitch function.) Return to the desired stitch setting, and **slowly stitch over the marked lines.** Secure the last stitch as you began. **Try a few different stitches for practice, comparison, and fun.**

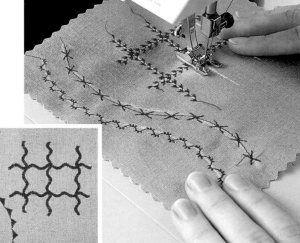

Altering Basic Stitches

1

Tip

You can stop your machine to adjust stitch width and length, or do it as you sew. Either method works!

Once you're comfortable with basic machine embroidery, broaden your horizons by experimenting with stitch lengths and widths. Select the basic zigzag stitch and begin by sewing it at the normal setting suggested by your machine's manual. Then, gradually adjust the stitch width, combining wide and narrow stitches in the same line of stitching. **Try this with both straight and wavy lines.** Or, contrast narrow and wide lines perpendicularly **to create your own machine-embroidered plaid.**

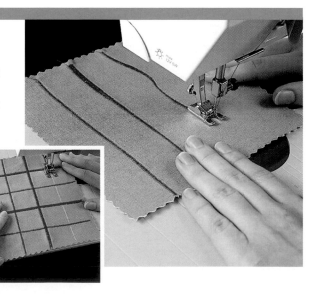

You can alter *any* stitch that zigzags, that is, any stitch with left-to-right needle motion. For example, select a blanket stitch or a simple herringbone variation, and sew it at the recommended machine setting in a straight line, and then a wavy one. For an interesting look, **experiment with changing the stitch width from wide to narrow and vice versa as you sew.**

Tip

Narrow or widen the stitch width *gradually,* to avoid abrupt changes in your lines of stitching.

Heavy Threads

Adjusting Bobbin Tension

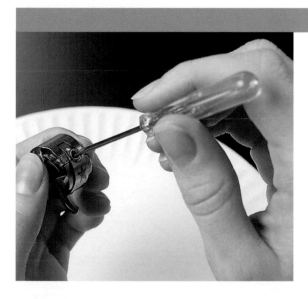

When working with heavier thread, you'll want to loosen the bobbin tension a bit. It's helpful to keep a second bobbin case handy with the tension preadjusted for thicker threads. (You can mark the latch with a permanent marker for identification purposes.) **To set the tension, use a screwdriver to turn the screw counterclockwise one-quarter rotation.** For heavy bobbin threads, continue to make one-quarter rotation turns until the thread pulls out smoothly, without resistance. Work over a plate, so you won't lose the screw should it fall out.

Tip

Remember this phrase for bobbin adjustments: Lefty-loosey, righty-tighty.

Heavy on Top

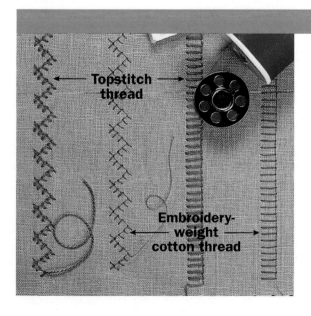

Topstitch thread

Embroidery-weight cotton thread

Heavier (thicker) decorative thread produces a visually stronger stitch than the same stitch sewn in embroidery-weight cotton or rayon. Topstitch, cordonnet, and the coarser, more textured metallics are all examples of heavier needle (top) threads. Topstitch threads require a needle with a larger eye, such as 130N, while metallics call for a Metallica or Metafil needle. Select a bobbin thread strong enough to support the heft of the heavier top thread. Metrolene (a strong, all-purpose bobbin thread) and polyester dressmaker's thread are both suitable choices.

MAGICAL MACHINE EMBROIDERY

45

Compatible Stitches

Decorative stitches, such as zigzag, blanket, and featherstitch, that don't incorporate backward and forward movements, are the best choices for heavier threads, like this topstitching and buttonhole twist thread. Set the stitch length for a longer-than-normal straight stitch (about 4), and play around with various widths. Always experiment, make adjustments, and make sure you are getting the effect you want on a practice sample before you try incorporating decorative stitching with thicker threads onto your quilt top.

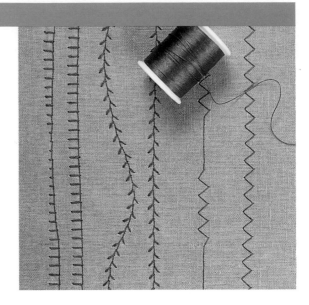

Heavy on the Bottom

If a thread is too thick or coarse to pass through the eye of the needle, you can sew from the wrong side of the fabric with the decorative thread in the bobbin. Pearl cotton, medium-weight metallics, thicker rayons, and narrow ribbon are all good choices for bobbinwork. Use a cotton or poly-ester dressmaker's thread in the needle. As you practice, adjust the top tension from 4 to 9. Mark the sample when you change from one tension setting to the next. **Examine the stitch quality you obtained for each setting, and select the best tension.**

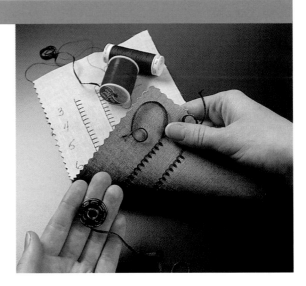

Variations on a Theme

Free-Motion Possibilities

Dropping or covering the machine's feed dogs allows you to move the fabric freely as you sew your favorite decorative stitches. You—not the machine—control the speed, direction, and shape of the stitch. Use a clear plastic darning foot or an open-toe foot for an unobstructed view. Select the desired decorative stitch, and begin sewing *slowly* at the inside of a marked spiral motif. Rotate the fabric so the needle creates a consistent stitch. **Follow the ever-widening, circular path for a graceful and interesting effect.**

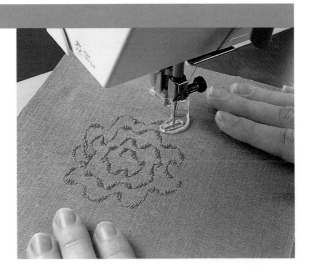

Open-Weave Distortions

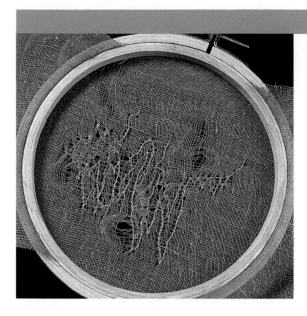

For interesting overlays for patches or for raw-edge appliqués loaded with texture, create interesting openwork in a gauzy, loosely woven fabric. First, stretch the fabric in a machine embroidery hoop. Thread the machine with lightweight cotton or metallic thread, select a simple decorative stitch, and sew across the fabric. If you wish, you can use the same free-motion techniques as before, and sew in a spiral again, or randomly back and forth, as shown here. **The decorative stitch opens and distorts the weave of the fabric.**

Tip

See "Adding Texture with Pintucks" on page 56 for lots more textural fabric manipulations.

Double-Needle Embroidery

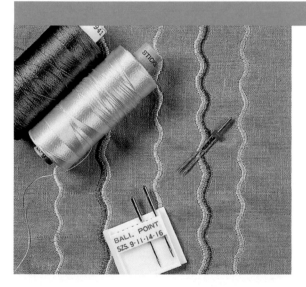

Here's a stitching option that's double the excitement! Select a decorative stitch, trying it out first with just one thread and a single needle. Insert a size 2.0 or 3.0 double needle in your sewing machine, and thread it with two contrasting-color threads of the same type. Refer to your manual for threading guidance; most machines can accommodate an alternate spool. Narrow the stitch width as necessary to accommodate the increased needle swing of the double needle. **Sew the same stitch with the double needle, and compare the results.**

Touching Stitches

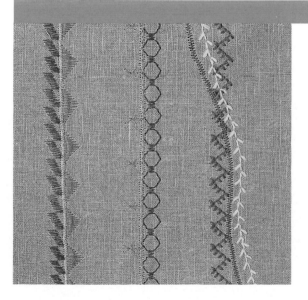

For the look of a rich, jacquard ribbon, sew a row of decorative stitches on stabilized fabric. Sew a second, complementary stitch to make a row that touches but doesn't overlap the first row of stitches. Adjust the stitch width to a narrow satin stitch (a width of about 2 should do it), and sew right down the center, between the two rows of stitches. This technique is effective with four or five touching rows as well. **Try it in various color combinations, and with rows of stitches that remain parallel or curve around each other.**

MAGICAL MACHINE EMBROIDERY

Creative Applications

Custom Yardage

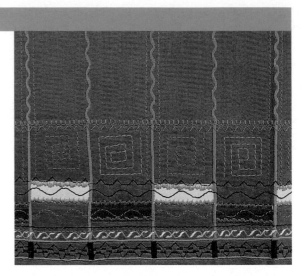

Tip

Jazz up your yardage by adding fused appliqués and satin-stitching the edges in coordinating or contrasting colors.

Combine all your favorite stitches into one large, wonderful piece of yardage. You might even find the result exciting enough for a wholecloth quilt or for use as a central medallion. Use combinations of patterns for large, open areas, such as wide borders or plain blocks. There's such a huge assortment of thread colors and textures available, you'll be able to coordinate your custom-made pieces to any colors or prints that you've already chosen to use.

Machine Appliqué in Bloom

Decorative embroidery can make machine appliqué positively blossom. Bond shapes to the background using fusible web or a spray-on fabric adhesive. Secure and finish the raw edges with a decorative stitch. A close zigzag (called the satin stitch) is the most common; buttonhole stitch is also very popular. Consult your sewing machine manual for other options. For the most durable finish, choose a stitch that covers the raw edge; the next best thing is a stitch with a spine (a straight line down the center or along one side).

Crazy Quilt Embellishment

Tip

Machine sew with every decorative stitch, color, and type of thread at your disposal, but add bugle and seed beads by hand; see page 26.

Decorative embroidery is the crowning touch of a Victorian-style crazy quilt. Now that you've practiced decorative embroidery with your machine, there's nothing to stop you from going crazy! Use speedy techniques such as foundation piecing or topstitch appliqué to make the quilt top; your decorative stitches will cover any topstitching. **Keep your work a manageable size: Stitch and frame one block to make a small quilt, like this 13 × 14-inch wall hanging,** or embellish several different blocks and assemble them for a "contained" crazy quilt of any size.

The Quilter's
Problem Solver

Treating Thread Traumas

Problem	Solution
The decorative stitch hardly shows after you've stitched it.	❑ Increase the contrast between thread and fabric by choosing a thread that is brighter, lighter, or darker. ❑ Switch to a more compact stitch (close zigzag or satin stitch, for example) so the stitch appears denser on the fabric. ❑ Use a contrasting thread to sew a second, complementary decorative stitch beside the first one. The contrast may make the first set of stitches more obvious.
The top thread shreds or breaks repeatedly.	Be sure you are using the proper needle type and size for your thread choice, and be sure that you have threaded the needle and wound and inserted the bobbin correctly. The thread may be twisted, feeding backward, or wrapping around the thread spindle, causing it to break. You may also need to loosen the top tension slightly for the thread to feed smoothly. If none of these solutions seem to help, discard the thread and try a newer or different spool. The thread may be brittle with age, or simply unsuitable for the job.
Your decorative stitches are tunneling and puckering.	❑ Have you remembered to stabilize your fabric? The typical quilt-weight cottons are usually too flimsy for successful machine embroidery without stabilizing. They may be stiffened with fusible interfacing or tear-away stabilizer. Even lightweight, silky yardage may be backed to make it usable. ❑ Be sure your top thread, bobbin thread, and needle are a good match, and replace worn needles frequently.

Skill Builder

Stripe it rich.

In addition to the "Touching Stitches" variation described on page 47, there are many other ways to create custom stripe-look fabrics for your quilts. Sew continuous rows of a favorite decorative stitch at 2-inch intervals. Then sew single repeats of another decorative stitch between the rows to create alternating stripes. Use your newly designed striped fabric for piecework (as the bars in a traditional Churn Dash, for example), for vertical and horizontal lattice, or as the sashing between rows in Flying Geese or other strippie-set quilt. You might also sew short, randomly spaced lines of one of the decorative stitches on another piece of the same fabric, and use the two coordinating fabrics together.

Try This!

Use the alphabet as a decorative stitch.

❑ Create "print" fabric. Use the programming feature on your machine or free-motion script to spell out names or favorite quotes on solid-color fabrics. Use the new fabrics as backgrounds for appliqués, or incorporate them into pieced blocks.

❑ Embroider names, places, or dates on ribbon, then attach the ribbon to your quilt with decorative stitching, buttons, or beads.

❑ Combine the alphabet with other decorative stitches to create attractive quilt labels.

MAGICAL MACHINE EMBROIDERY

49

H
ave you been longing to use those neat rubber stamps on your quilts? Would you
love to design one-of-a-kind fabrics for your next project? Well, wish no longer!
With a few stamps, a splash of textile paint or ink, and a touch of imagination, you
can transform commercial fabrics and your quilts with rubber-stamping expertise. Whether
you favor overall or asymmetrical designs or special words and phrases, you'll find stamping to
be quick, creative, and fun. And there's no drawing skill or math required. Just don a smock,
roll up your sleeves, and create your own rubber-stamped masterpiece!

Getting Ready

Light-color, tightly woven, 100 percent cotton fabrics such as Pima cotton, cotton lawn, or quality muslin work best for stamping, enabling you to achieve clear, crisp images. Be sure to prewash and dry all fabrics, and iron them if necessary.

Big, bold, deeply etched stamps are easy to use and give the best results on fabric. Pair these with colorfast paints and inks designed specifically for use on cloth. Assess your personal preferences regarding cost, convenience, and creativity to decide between paints and inks. Paints, sold by the jar, are usually less expensive, allow you to mix colors, and sometimes provide better coverage. On the other hand, pre-inked pads are more convenient and generally less messy to use—simply remove the lid and you're ready to go. And if you're working with more intricately carved stamp designs, you'll probably get better, more even results with an inkpad. Check your local quilt or craft shop to explore the wide range of options available.

Steps for Successful Stamping

1

Cover your work surface with newspaper, flattened paper bags, a vinyl tablecloth, or a plastic dropcloth.

Place your prewashed fabric right side up on a flat, slightly padded surface. A few neatly stacked newspapers or flattened brown grocery bags provide just enough padding for good stamping results. If you're stamping a large piece of fabric, particularly one that extends over the edges of your stamping surface, **clamp the fabric to the surface with clothespins** or bulldog clips to prevent the fabric from shifting.

Tip

If you don't have clothespins or bulldog clips handy, weight down the corners of your fabric with canned goods.

2

The stamping medium you select will
determine the method you use for
preparing your stamps. **If you're using
fabric paint, apply it directly to the
surface of the rubber stamp using a
small (1-inch) foam paintbrush** or a
wedge-shaped cosmetic sponge.
Long, even brush strokes give the
best coverage.

3

If you're using a pre-inked fabric
stamp pad, **lightly tap the rubber
stamp on the pad's surface.** Don't
press the stamp into the pad; exces-
sive pressure causes the stamp to take
on too much ink. This can cause the
resulting image to smear or
"shadow" around its outside edges. If
there are areas that don't have ink on
them, tap the stamp on the
pad again. **If there is too
much ink, clean some off
with a cotton swab,** or
"stamp off" the excess on a
scrap of cloth or paper.

4

**Press the painted or inked stamp onto
the fabric with a steady hand, applying even pressure to the back of
the stamp mount.** This is especially
important with larger stamps. While
you'll want to apply adequate pressure to transfer the paint to the
fabric, pressing too hard may cause
the paint to ooze out from under the
stamp and concentrate around the
stamp's edges. Also, don't wiggle or
rock the stamp back and forth, or the
image might smear. With a little practice, you'll discover the correct
amount of pressure to use to achieve
the best results.

Hold the fabric in place with one hand (be sure you don't have any paint on your fingertips first!) as you **lift the stamp straight up with the other hand.**

You'll have the most fun if you **stamp images randomly onto the fabric and don't worry about lining them up.** To maximize visual interest, stamp the image a few times before re-inking the stamp. Each successive image will be lighter in value than the previous one, creating interesting and dramatic textures. For even more interest, vary the colors or shades of ink you use. If you are stamping natural motifs, vary the colors in subsequent stamps, or **combine two or more colors on a single stamp.** For example, blend pink into purple for blossom petals.

Keep a box of folded, premoistened wipes opened nearby as you work. When you're finished with a particular stamp or you wish to change to a different paint or ink color, **clean the stamp by "stamping off" the pigment onto the top wipe in the box.** Discard this wipe when it gets covered with paint.

When you're finished stamping for the day, thoroughly clean all of your stamps by rinsing them in warm water. **An old toothbrush and mild dish detergent are great for removing dried or stubborn paint.**

Tip

Stamp off excess ink on a scrap piece of fabric. You might end up with a wonderful unplanned design of colors and images!

STAMPS OF APPROVAL

Tip

You can also heat set stamped fabrics by tumbling them for 30 minutes in a commercial clothes dryer. (Household dryers don't get hot enough.)

Refer to the instructions on the paint jar or stamp pad to set your stamped images. If there are no specific instructions on the product, allow the ink to dry for at least 24 hours. Then set a dry iron to the hottest temperature appropriate for the fabric you're using, and protect your ironing surface with paper towels. Place the stamped fabric wrong side up on the protected surface, and cover it with a press cloth. **Press each stamped image for 60 seconds, moving the iron over the fabric to prevent scorching.**

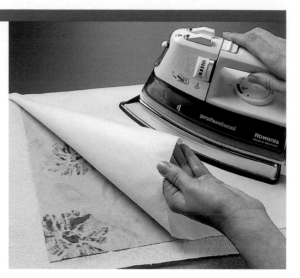

Beyond the Basics

Lettering

Tip

Use a light box along with your stamping guide to align and space letters on dark fabric.

You can include names, words, or special phrases on your quilt. Line up figures neatly for a formal appearance or stagger them for a playful look. Cut pieces of paper the same size as the area you're stamping and **practice until the letters or words fit the area.** For controlled spacing, make a stamping guide using lined paper. Darken lines with a marker, and place the guide under the paper or fabric. **Or, simply cut a margin around your best stamping examples and create a quilt around them!**

Found Materials

You needn't break the bank collecting commercially produced stamps. A quick look around the house will provide a wealth of creative stamping materials. **Experiment with bubble wrap, empty thread spools,** cut fruits and vegetables, leaves, shells, clean sneaker treads, chicken wire, foam or Styrofoam shapes, wood blocks, finger or hand prints (yours, your spouse's, or your children's), corks, and old keys. These will give wonderful, one-of-a-kind, and economical results. Or, carve your own designs into artist's erasers or potatoes.

The Quilter's
Problem Solver

Stamp Out Problems

Problem	Solution
The fabric keeps shifting as you stamp it.	Stabilize it with freezer paper. Use a hot iron to press the waxy side of the paper to the wrong side of the fabric. After you have finished stamping and the paints have completely dried (but are not yet heat set), remove the freezer paper and proceed as usual.
You want to stamp on dark fabric but worry that the paint won't show.	While it's true that most fabric paints show up only when stamped on lighter fabric, there are ways around this problem. Look for a fabric paint that is labeled *opaque*. Some brands make an *opaque* or *covering white* that you can mix with other colors to use on dark fabrics. Follow the manufacturer's instructions for best results.

Build confidence with creative practice!

If you've never stamped before and are nervous about "messing up" your fabric, practice on a T-shirt, sweatshirt, or child's garment to gain confidence. You can even breathe new life into a less-than-new garment by stamping over stubborn stains!

Try This!

Plan ahead to minimize cleanup.

When you're planning an extensive stamping session and will be using lots of different stamps, fill an old cookie sheet with $1/16$ inch of water and place it near your work surface. As you finish with each stamp, place it rubber side down in the pan. (Be sure the water doesn't touch the wooden stamp mount, or you might damage the wood or loosen the adhesive that bonds it to the stamp.) The paint won't be able to dry on the stamp, making it much easier to clean up when you're finished for the day.

STAMPS OF APPROVAL

55

Adding Texture
with Pintucks

Here's a nifty technique, borrowed from dressmakers, to tuck into your embellisher's bag of tricks. Introduce rows of sliver-thin pleats, or pintucks, into some ordinary fat-eighths or fat-quarters. Suddenly you have wonderful, textural fabrics at your disposal, to add special effects to patchwork, appliqué, quilts, and wearables. Pintucking is fairly effortless to do on your sewing machine, once you're armed with a twin needle; a special, grooved presser foot; and some leisure time to practice and experiment.

Getting Ready

You'll need a pintuck foot with 5 or 7 grooves for pintucking quilt-weight cotton fabrics. Most sewing machine manufacturers make them to fit their machines.

Consult your sewing machine manual, and select a twin or double needle to fit the foot. You'll see two numbers on the needle packaging. The first indicates the distance in millimeters between the needles (2.0, 2.5, 3.0, and so on). The higher the number, the wider the spacing, and the wider the spacing, the larger the tuck. The second number indicates the needle size; choose a size 80 or 90 for pintucking most quilting cottons.

Cotton embroidery thread lends a traditional appearance; rayon, polyester, and acrylics add extra shine; and metallic, iridescent, and opalescent threads infuse a touch of glamour. You'll need an alternate spool holder, to hold a second spool of thread for the double needle, and to make corded pintucks, you'll need a thin cord such as gimp. If what you're using isn't the Mettler product called for herc, be sure to prewash and preshrink it.

Pintuck Pointers

Machine Setup

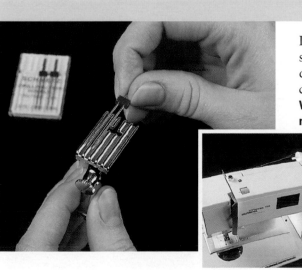

Install the pintuck foot, alternate spool holder, and twin needle. The distance between the needles must correspond to the grooves in the foot. **When the needle and foot are properly matched, a needle will sit in the center of two adjoining grooves.** Thread the twin needles with a lightweight thread. **Use the left or lower spool holder and left tension disk to thread the left needle and the right or upper spool holder and right tension disk for the right needle.**

Tip

For pintucking, use a lightweight thread in the bobbin of your machine.

Basic Pintucking

Work with a 9-inch fabric square for practice. Align the lengthwise raw edge with the 1-inch throatplate marking to the right of the needle. **Begin stitching, and watch a pintuck form!** When you reach the end of the fabric, raise the needle, turn the fabric around and go back the other way. **Slide the completed row of stitches under the last groove in the foot, and begin stitching another pintuck.** To keep all your rows straight and evenly spaced, use the same grooves throughout.

Tip

If you're going to make lots of pintucks, start with a piece of fabric that is twice as wide as the desired finished fabric.

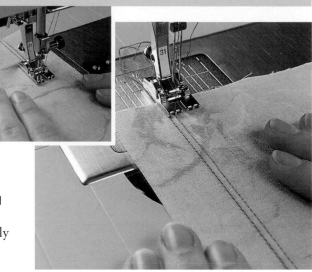

Corded Pintucks

Cording gives a crisper, rounder look to the finished pintuck. To make corded pintucks, lower the feed dogs, remove the bobbin case and throatplate, and **slide the end of a spool of gimp up through the bobbin area and through the hole in the throatplate.** Be careful not to tangle the gimp in the feed dogs. Hold on to the tail and raise the feed dogs to sew, leaving the bobbin door open. Turn the fabric around for each row to save gimp, thread, and time clipping thread ends.

Tip

Place the spool of gimp on a freestanding spool stand to lessen kinks and twists.

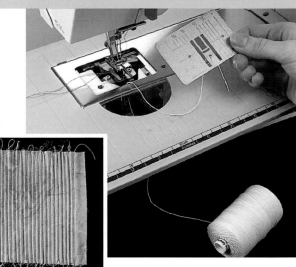

Pintucks in the Round

If your sewing machine has a free arm, pintucking in the round saves time and thread. Use a 9 × 18-inch piece of fabric. Stitch the short edges right sides together with a ¼ inch seam, forming a tube. **Align the lengthwise raw edge with a throatplate marking and, beginning at the seam,** stitch completely around the tube. At the seam, raise the needle, slide the pintuck **to nestle along the right side of the foot, and stitch around again.** When the desired number of rounds are sewn, cut the tube open along the seam.

Tip

If you offset the fabric edges in the tube seam by the desired distance between tucks, then you can sew pintucks in continuous spirals.

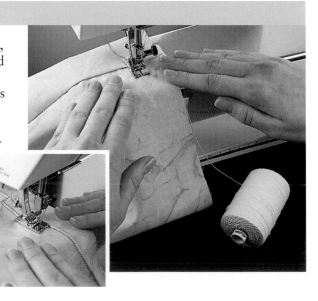

Pintuck Possibilities

Once you feel confident with the basic pintucking technique, **experiment with some different spacing and line formations.** Stitch pintucks in groups, using a seam guide on your machine to keep the spacing consistent. Cross your pintucks with intersecting lines. Try stitching wavy rows. You can also mark a gentle scallop for lovely, parallel pintucks along the border strips for a Baltimore Album quilt. For best results, keep to straight lines or gentle curves; don't try designs that require sharp turns or tight curves.

Tip

Use a different color of thread for each needle, or try two spools of the same variegated thread.

Piecing with Tucked Fabric

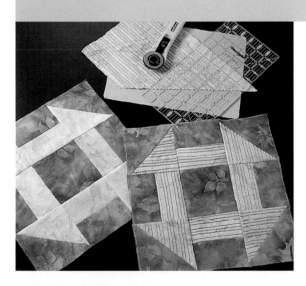

Treat your pintucked results as specialty fabric, and use it to cut patches, alternate blocks, corner squares, and other elements for your pieced quilt or garment. **Pintucking will add texture and panache to even the most traditional quilt pattern.** Press your pintucked pieces before cutting them, and remember to add ¼-inch seam allowances when cutting. Do a little planning to avoid the excess bulk that would result at intersections of multiple seam allowances that contain pintucks. Avoid corded pintucks for patchwork.

Tip

For added detail, stitch contrasting-color piping between the pintucked pieces.

Pintuck Appliqués

Appliqués made from pintucked fabric add exciting dimension and texture. Machine appliqué is your best bet for stitching them to the background because the tucks are too bulky to turn under. Cut the appliqué to the desired finished size. Position it on the quilt top. Pin or use fusible web to hold the appliqué in place. Attach an open-toe foot to your machine, use a tear-away stabilizer under the fabric, and use an open zigzag stitch or other decorative stitch to completely cover the raw edges. You may need to stitch around the appliqué more than once.

ADDING TEXTURE WITH PINTUCKS

Lacey
& Lovely

ransform your sewing machine doodles into lofty works of art with this heavenly free-motion technique for creating airy, lacelike appliqués! With just a bit of heat-sensitive stabilizer and your favorite threads, you'll soon be fashioning gossamer angel wings, frothy foam, lacy foliage, and puffy clouds that seem to float across your quilt top. Follow the simple, step-by-step instructions in this chapter, and lift your embellishing skills to new heights in no time at all!

Getting Ready

Sulky Heat Away, a stabilizer that disappears when heated with an iron, is essential to the success of this technique. It comes in only one weight and is available at most sewing and quilting shops.

Simple appliqué patterns, children's artwork, and coloring-book drawings make excellent design sources for lace motifs. If you're making organic treetops, shrubs, or clouds, you can draw your pattern freehand. In any case, use at least two different decorative threads to create your design. The rich, dense colors of Sulky Rayon create a strong, solid thread line, perfect for outlining. An acrylic embroidery thread, such as a variegated YLI Ultrasheen, is a good option for filling in the design. Even though these threads are opaque, the openwork stitching creates an ethereal, transparent effect.

What You'll Need

Medium-point, permanent black fabric marker

Appliqué or other commercial patterns, children's artwork, or coloring books

Sulky Heat Away stabilizer

8- or 10-inch machine embroidery hoop

Ivory tulle or fine netting

Various decorative threads, such as Sulky Rayon and YLI Ultrasheen

90/14 machine-embroidery needles

Darning foot

Iron and ironing surface

Sewing machine

Creating Lace Motifs

1

Use a medium-point, permanent black fabric marker to trace your chosen design onto a piece of Sulky Heat Away stabilizer. You should be able to see the pattern through the stabilizer, but you can use a light box if necessary.

The size of your embroidery hoop will determine how large to cut the stabilizer. If your design fits inside the hoop, cut the stabilizer at least 3 inches larger than the hoop. If the design is larger than the hoop, cut the stabilizer at least 3 inches larger than the design. Cut and mark a second piece of stabilizer to use for practice.

Tip

Outline your original pattern with a black marking pen to make it easier to see while tracing.

L A C E Y & L O V E L Y

2

Cut two pieces of ivory tulle or fine netting the same size as the marked stabilizer. (A dark-color tulle is used here for better visibility.) **Center one piece of the tulle over one piece of marked stabilizer (pattern side up),** and place the layers in the machine embroidery hoop, aligning the recessed areas of the inner and outer hoops. **Make sure the layers are flush with the tabletop.** Tighten the screw so both the netting and stabilizer are taut in the hoop. This will be your practice piece.

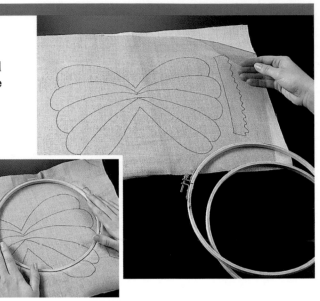

3

Thread your machine and bobbin with the thread you've chosen to fill in the design. Lower or cover the feed dogs on your machine. Insert a size 90/14 machine embroidery needle, attach the darning foot, and loosen the upper tension slightly. Practice free-motion stitching on your sample until you achieve a fairly consistent stitch length. **Fill in the design first, moving the hoop in ¼-inch circles to produce dense, overlapping curlicues and loops.** When you've mastered that motion, practice outlining the motif. Proceed to your second marked design as soon as you feel confident.

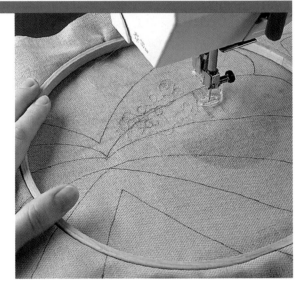

4

As you make the move from your practice to your "real" piece, begin by outlining your design. For an obvious, dramatic outline, thread your machine with a heavier thread in a darker color. **Free-motion stitch around the marked outlines and other key lines of the design that you've drawn.** Go over these lines two, three, or four times, stacking the lines of stitching on top of each other to create the look of one heavy, solid line. Work in this manner over one area at a time, to avoid frequently repositioning the hoop.

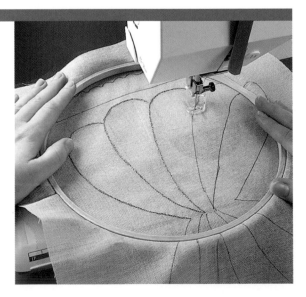

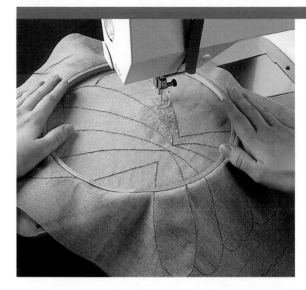

5

Next, change the needle and bobbin thread to the thread you've chosen to fill in the design.

Begin filling up the areas within the outlines of the design, moving the hoop in small circles, as you did on your practice piece. Ignore key interior lines, such as veins, and simply stitch over them.

Try combining threads of different colors or values. The layering will cause them to blend naturally.

Cut out the lace motif, leaving a tiny bit of stabilizer around the outer edges.

Set a dry iron to a high cotton setting. Use the iron directly on the Sulky Heat Away lace motif until the stabilizer begins to turn brown (10 to 15 seconds). Don't let the lace get too hot or leave the iron sitting on it, as the tulle will melt. **Once all the areas of the stabilizer have darkened, gently rub and crinkle the lace motif in your hand.** The stabilizer will disintegrate, leaving only the netting and network of thread.

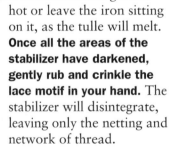

Use a soft-bristled toothbrush to gently brush away stubborn bits of darkened Sulky Heat Away.

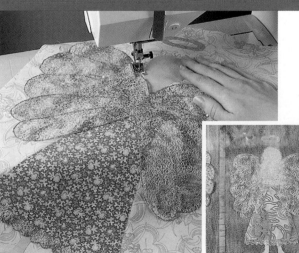

7

Use a narrow zigzag (satin) stitch to attach the lace motif to your quilt, using the same thread you used to outline the motif in Step 4 on the opposite page. Stitch along the outlined edges of the design or along key lines or "veins." **Consider leaving part of the design unattached for a dimensional effect.**

L A C E Y & L O V E L Y

Innovative
Trimmings

I f you're ready to move beyond buttons and beads, then this chapter is for you! Perhaps you've encountered a most intriguing item, or you want to add seashells to your quilt, but you're wondering "How in the world do I do that?" Whether romantic or funky, opulent or offbeat, high-style or high-tech, these techniques for attaching out-of-the-ordinary trims and trinkets help you rise to the challenge. Although they seem tricky at first glance, these visual treats are easy to find and to attach—one way or another.

Getting Ready

As you consider working with quirky embellishments, it's important to understand their special needs. Give careful thought to the color and type of thread you use to attach the item. If you prefer that the thread not show, decide if you should match the thread to the item or the background fabric. *Always* use cotton to attach fragile vintage fabrics, laces, or ribbons, which may not endure abrasion from synthetic threads. If the fabrics and trims are new and sturdy, however, experiment with metallics, silk buttonhole twist, or other shiny threads or flosses for accent or contrast. If you must press unusual mesh ribbons and specialty trims before (or after) applying them, carefully adjust the iron's temperature to accommodate the fiber content of the particular item. If it becomes absolutely necessary to wash the quilt, protect delicate or fragile embellishments, such as tiny shells, by basting over them with muslin or voile before immersing them in a cool-water soak. And avoid scrubbing, which can tarnish or weaken certain decorative threads and trims.

What You'll Need

- **Fabric, craft, and embroidery scissors**
- **Variety of fabric glues, epoxies, and adhesives**
- **Decorative threads, ribbons, and trims**
- **Beads, buttons, and trinkets**
- **Pompoms and chenille sticks**
- **Velvet leaves and silk flowers**
- **Filigrees**
- **Millinery and bridal lace**
- **Fabric paint and brushes**
- **Nuts, bolts, and electrical components**
- **Buckles**
- **Shells and natural objects**
- **Coins, tokens, and bottle caps**

Choose the Unusual

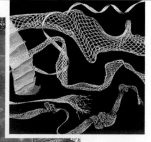

Metallic Mesh

Look for a wide assortment of metallic netting and mesh ribbons at craft stores and floral shops, as well as at your favorite fabric haunts. These versatile trims have a malleability that is intriguing and fun. **Twist them, pull them apart, coax them into curves,** fold them into accordion-pleats, or cut them into pieces for glitzy, see-through accents. Tack them in place by hand or machine, before or after quilting, or couch them along their sides, down the middle, or across their entire width.

Wire-Edge Ribbon

Tip

Use wire-edge ribbon to make variegated roses; see page 78.

Another flexible, fun-to-use ribbon has wire along the edges only. These ribbons are popular with quiltmakers who like their **bows to have soft, lazy loops and undulating streamers that won't fall flat.** Tack dimensional, wire-edge creations on projects that will get minimal wear and are unlikely to be flattened. Also, consider alternative, less-fragile uses for wire-edge ribbon, such as **gathering it into curves or coils by gently sliding the ribbon along one or both wire edges.** Look for this ribbon at craft, floral, and fabric stores.

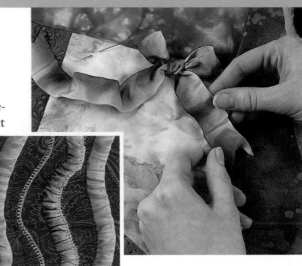

Sequin Waste

Tip

Take care that you don't fold your quilt along sequin waste; any creases in the trim will become permanent.

Also know as punchinello, sequin waste is the ribbonlike trim that remains after the sequins have been punched out. It is sold by the yard in craft and fabric stores, and it can be used much as you would any other decorative trim—for added texture and visual interest with a modernistic and somewhat funky twist. **It is easily cut into small pieces with craft scissors, and it can either be glued with a strong, permanent fabric glue** or hand stitched in place.

Specialty Ribbons

Tip

Dip sections of purchased rayon ribbon or rayon seam bindings into cups of dye for a beautiful, variegated look.

Vintage, hand-dyed, or imported ribbons can be found at antique shows, flea markets, and quilt shows. Whether rayon or silk, plain-weave or enhanced with intricate, jacquard designs, these ribbons add a unique accent to your quilts. Appliqué them along their edges or couch them with decorative threads. Delicate, 1/4-inch-wide rayon ribbon or bias tape can be teased into gentle curves or ruched using a strong thread. Either way, **why not tack it in place with seed beads?**

Buckles

Buckles provide flat but interesting shapes, opening the door to aesthetic possibilities that far exceed their utilitarian purpose. In addition to the more standard fasteners, explore the potential of D-rings, overall strap buckles, lingerie fasteners, and knotted frog closures. You'll find all of these eye-catching trinkets in a well-stocked notions department or at your favorite craft supply store. **For extra panache, thread ribbons through the shanks of buckles.**

Tip

Hand stitch buckles and fasteners in matching thread for less impact, or use high-contrast or sparkly thread for added pizzazz.

Washers & Tokens

Buckles are not the only functional items that offer the advantage of sew-through ease. Consider the many diminutive disks that you routinely encounter, many with center holes just right for stitching. **Think washers and nuts from the hardware store, subway or toll tokens, and even some foreign coins.** Attach these securely by hand, stitching over the edges. Imagine the ring as a clockface, and **make stitches at 12, 2, 4, 6, 8, and 10 o'clock, or at other evenly spaced intervals.**

Filigree & Rondels

Lacy metal filigrees may be found in stores that carry beads and jewelry-making supplies, or perhaps among your own broken or cast-off jewelry. Likewise, you will probably find rondels—flat, round beads made of glass, plastic, or metal, with holes in the centers. Hand stitch over the edges or through the holes in these items to hold them in place. **Combine filigrees and rondels together,** or accent the pieces separately with seed beads or metallic threads.

INNOVATIVE TRIMMINGS

67

Velvet Leaves & Silk Flowers

Tip

Scout flea markets for vintage corsages of silk flowers that have seen better days; recycle the usable parts.

Velvet leaves add a rich, old-fashioned look when paired with silk flowers, or those made from porcelain or coiled ribbons. The wire veins usually peel right off if you wish to remove them for a softer look and feel. Tack the leaves to the background fabric with beads or thread, or run a hand- or machine-embroidery stitch up the center vein, continuing on to form a stem. In addition to velvet leaves, **search craft stores for leaves in other textures, as well as for stamens** and silk flowers—the smaller and flatter, the better.

Millinery & Bridal Motifs

Tip

Coat the edges of "fuzzy" or raveling appliqués with a fabric sealant such as FrayCheck.

A trip to the millinery or bridal section of a fabric shop can yield a wealth of creative embellishment materials. Tiny floral sprays can fill a pieced basket to overflowing or dot the landscape of a fabric garden. Lace appliqués appear to float on the surface of a quilt when tacked along their edges. **Enhance their impact with a wash of water-thinned fabric paint.** Glue-baste if desired, and then tack or appliqué these items in place. Add colorful embroidery stitches, or stud them with pearls or crystals to highlight areas of the design.

Shells as Beads

Tip

Many bead shops offer coral beads in carved or natural forms.

A stroll along the beach may reward you with **tiny shells already sporting holes perfect for stitching through.** In addition, import or craft shops often carry cowrie shells, starfish, and more. Whether whole shells, shell slices, or tiny pieces, these souvenirs from the sea often feature branching forms or thin, extending elements that make them easy to attach with a few tacking stitches and strong thread. **Sprinkle them randomly across your quilt top for natural texture.**

Small Scallop Shells

What if your seaside collectibles lack holes or other stitchable features? Drilling holes in such fragile treasures is definitely risky. Instead, take this tip from quilt artist Marguerite Malwitz: **Use strong epoxy to glue a small, plastic, shank-type button to the shell's concave surface.** A plastic mother-of-pearl button ensures no shadow-through for an airy, delicately colored scallop shell; we used a contrasting button here for visibility. You can sew the shell-button onto your quilt as soon as the glue is dry.

Tip

Use shank buttons to create your own novelty buttons from coins, bottle caps, and other small, found objects.

Pompoms

The humble pompom just might provide the ideal touch of soft, matte texture for a very special quilt. In Janeene Herchold's dramatic wall piece, **pompoms accentuate the curve of a sunflower petal,** perfectly suggesting its downy, velvety surface. Pompoms come in a variety of colors and sizes. Whether you **dot a design with individual pompoms, line them up, or cluster them densely,** use a good glue with a thin applicator tip to permanently secure them to your quilt. Test the product first (see "Skill Builder" on page 71.)

Tip

Cluster pompoms together to create warm and fuzzy chicks, lambs, or poodles.

Chenille Sticks

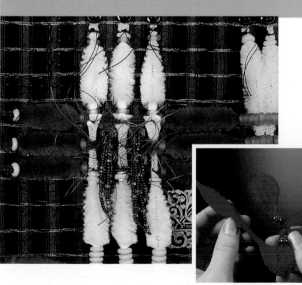

That other mainstay of inexpensive crafts, the pipe cleaner, may also find new life in the hands of an enterprising quilt embellisher. Also known as chenille sticks, pipe cleaners may be found in an intriguing thick-and-thin combination, called bumpy chenille sticks or chenille bumps. **Thread pony beads onto them,** cross or weave them, and then couch or tie them to secure them to your quilt surface. Of course, their wire base means that **you can also bend them into flowers, or any other shape you want.**

Electrical Supplies

Tip

For a closer look at the innovative trims found on this quilt, turn to the page opposite the copyright page.

Hardware, home repair, and electronics stores are great sources for offbeat, high-tech embellishments. **To finish her quilt titled "Power Surge," Ginette Bourque used an electric plug!** She replaced the plastic cord with a softer, round rayon cord, which she then appliquéd in place along the binding's zigzag path. In keeping with her high-powered theme, Ginette incorporated alligator clips as arms and legs for one of the robots (second row, left.)

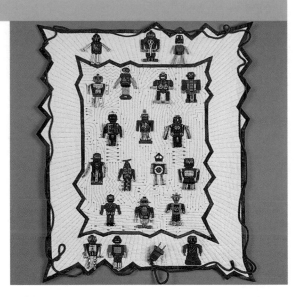

Recyclables

Little metal notions may be just the ticket for sending your quilt design into orbit. **Take inspiration from the unusual embellishments shown here:** The robot on the left has hardware nuts as eyes, as dials on his chest, and strung together to make legs. Screws adorn his midsection, and miniature tools from the dollhouse store serve as arms. His colleague has little, low-voltage wire connectors (found with electrical supplies) for hands and feet and a piece of wire screen mesh as a monitor-screen abdomen.

Jewelry Box Treasures

Embellishments needn't be new to be effective. Search your jewelry box for **earrings that have lost their mates, broken bracelets and necklaces, and non-functioning wristwatches.** Take these and similar items apart, and salvage the pieces. **In this fleet of robots, you'll see watch parts and the springs from old, used-up ballpoint pens. There are also small microchips taken from a computer board on the scrap heap.** Put all manner of odd notions to good use as embellishments: safety pins, snaps, and jingle bells. Attach them with decorative thread or seed beads.

The Quilter's Problem Solver

Putting Paper Mementoes into a Quilt

Problem	Solution
You have some unusual, highly personal paper items you'd like to include in a family album or birthday quilt. How can you attach seed packets, postcards, or even expired library cards, short of transferring the images to fabric?	Consider this the perfect opportunity to hone all of your embellishing skills! Try some (or all) of the following: ❏ Cover your flat embellishments with tulle or netting, stitched or couched around the edges with decorative trim or see page 82 to learn how to make a vinyl overlay. ❏ If you'd rather avoid overlays, use a small (⅛- or ¹⁄₁₆-inch) hole punch or ice pick to make holes in the item, and secure it with whipstitches, colorful ties, stitched-on buttons, or beads. ❏ Thread a narrow silk ribbon onto a chenille needle and fix the item to the quilt "gift package" style, stitching over it in a large "+" or "x" and finishing with a perky bow.

see page 82

Skill Builder

Learn the what, where, and when info on glues.

Always test a particular fabric glue or epoxy on the fabrics and embellishments you're using for that project, even if you've used the adhesive successfully before. Sometimes it is the combination of items being adhered, not the adhesive itself, that causes the problem. Some glues can damage or discolor certain fabrics or trims while being perfectly harmless to others. Better to be safe than sorry!

Try This!

Adopt an orphan.

Embellishment, that is! Orphaned doll and dollhouse accessories, game pieces, unused holiday decorations, and outdated pet tags are all fair game for the innovative embellisher. Depending upon the weight of the item and whether or not it has holes or loops, you can use fabric glue or epoxy, thread, yarn, floss, ribbon, buttons, or beads to secure it in place.

INNOVATIVE TRIMMINGS

71

A Garden
of Flowers

Infuse your quilts with pure romance as you stitch fanciful flowers and glorious greenery onto them. Gathered, rolled, and slashed fabric scraps mix with gradated ribbons and trims to give these floral embellishments texture and depth. Let these lovely blossoms inspire you to create your own arrangements. Change the scale; mix and match the petals, centers, stems, and leaves; and add your own finishing touches. Every quiltmaker has a green thumb for these easy blooms!

Getting Ready

This chapter shows you how to make five different dimensional flowers. Use them as embellishment for quilts or garments, or substitute them for similar flowers in your favorite two-dimensional appliqué designs.

While the delicately colored silk and grosgrain ribbons shown in the photos suggest a romantic Baltimore Album look, they're easily replaced with ginghams or natural, unbleached linen or cotton, for a more homespun appearance. Use sturdy quilting thread (or a double strand of sewing thread) for gathering stitches, but a fine sewing thread such as Mettler 60/2 for appliqué. You can use any decorative thread to add detail and texture. Note that we used contrasting thread in many of the photographs to make the stitching more visible, but you'll want to use thread that matches or complements the color of your embellishment.

Be sure your work surface is protected. A large piece of freezer paper turned waxy side up and secured with masking tape allows fabric shapes to peel off easily, even after they have been treated with sealants or fabric glue.

What You'll Need

- **Background fabric or quilt top**
- **Braids, ribbons, and trims**
- **Scissors for fabric, paper, and embroidery**
- **Water-soluble fabric glue**
- **Sewing and embroidery needles**
- **Functional and decorative threads and flosses**
- **Lightweight fusible web**
- **Template plastic**
- **Fabric marker**
- **Fabric sealant**
- **Prewashed fabric scraps**
- **Spray or liquid starch**
- **Clover Bias Maker #6, ¼ inch wide**
- **Crochet hook**
- **Compass or circle guide**

Scottish Thistle

1

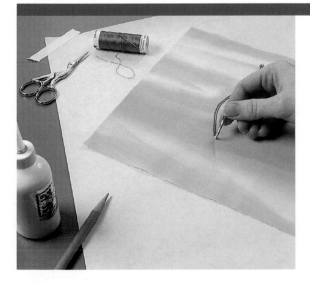

Soutache braid makes great stems: It's flexible, elegant, textural, available in various widths, and the edges are finished. Draw a graceful line for the stem on the background fabric. Cut the braid to the length of the marked line, adding a little extra at the end that will be overlapped by the thistle.

Place the braid right side down on a protected work surface, and run a thin line of fabric glue along the back. **Position the braid glue side down on the background fabric,** allow the glue to dry, and secure it permanently by hand or machine.

Tip

Rule of green thumb: Apply stems first, so you can hide the raw ends with leaves and flower heads.

A GARDEN OF FLOWERS

2

The thistle leaf is double-sided and is secured by stitching down the middle. Cut a 3-inch square from two green fabrics and a slightly smaller square of fusible web. Follow the instructions to fuse the web to the wrong side of one fabric, peel away the paper backing, and fuse to the wrong side of the other fabric. Trace the Scottish Thistle Leaf pattern on page 79 onto template plastic and cut it out to make a template. **Use a fabric marker to trace around the template on one side of the bonded fabric.** Cut out the leaf just inside the marked lines.

Tip

For natural diversity, use templates cut from freezer paper to make individual leaf shapes, each slightly different.

3

To prevent the raw edges from fraying, use a fabric sealant such as Fray Check. Working on a protected surface, **apply the sealant to the raw edges of the leaves.** When they are dry, position them on the background. **Attach them by machine stitching down the center of each leaf, connecting the leaf to the stem in the process.** Or, attach the leaves by hand: Stab stitch down the center with two strands of green embroidery floss. In either case, leave the leaf edges free.

Tip

Add a pattern of veins to your leaves with a permanent marker in a darker shade of green.

4

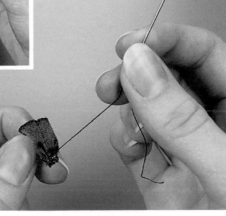

Make the thistle pod from a stuffed tube of ribbon. Cut a 1½-inch length of ⅝-inch-wide green ribbon. (Remove the wire if you are using a wire-edge ribbon.) Fold the ribbon in half crosswise, wrong side out, so the short raw edges meet. **Sew a straight stitch about ¼ inch from the raw edges to form a small tube,** and turn the ribbon right side out. Use matching thread to sew a running stitch along one end of the tube, just inside the selvage. **Pull the thread to gather the tube tightly, closing the bottom end of the pod;** backstitch to fasten securely.

Tip

Make a large bud or dimensional flower center in the same way, stuffing the center with a small piece of batting and gathering both ends tightly.

For the silky blossom that emerges from the thistle pod, use grosgrain ribbon that's at least ⅞ inch wide. Cut a 4-inch piece and remove one long edge, leaving it ¾ inch wide, with one selvage intact. Unravel the lengthwise threads until the woven area is ¼ inch wide. **Wind the ribbon into a tight coil along the selvage,** securing with tacking stitches. Glue the coil inside the thistle pod so just the fringe shows. Appliqué the pod to the background, over the stem end, **letting the fringe extend outward freely.**

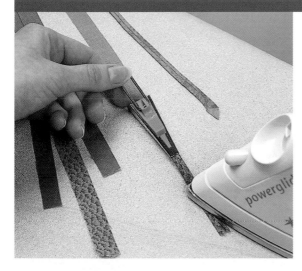

Tip

Use a pin to pick out threads along the long edge of the ribbon when you fringe your thistle blossom.

Pansy

1

To make finished ¼-inch-wide bias strip stems, cut ¾-inch-wide bias strips that are ½ inch longer than the desired finished stem. Starch each strip, then, while it's still wet, **draw the strip through a bias maker, pressing the folds as they are made.** Turn under the end that won't be overlapped by a flower head, and press. Apply fabric glue to the back of the stem, and glue it to the background fabric. When the glue is dry, hand or machine appliqué the stem with matching thread.

Tip

For a dimensional look, use a blunt tapestry needle to run yarn through the appliquéd stems.

2

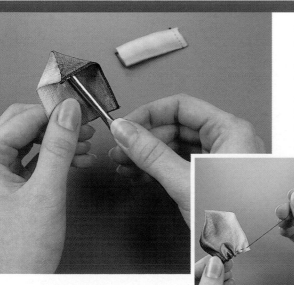

To make a leaf, start with 2-inch lengths of 1⅜-inch-wide green wire-edge ribbon. Fold it in half length-wise, right sides together. Using matching thread and starting at the fold, stitch a ¼-inch seam across one short, raw edge. Begin and end with a knot. Turn the ribbon right side out, and **use a crochet hook to form the leaf point.** Then run a gathering stitch along the opposite cut edge, and **draw the leaf end together.** Secure with a knot. Pin, then appliqué the leaf in place.

Tip

Cut a longer length of ribbon, and use this technique to make leaves for tulips, daffodils, or irises.

A GARDEN OF FLOWERS

3

For the flower, trace the Pansy Flower Top Petal A pattern on page 79 onto template plastic. Use a compass or circle guide to mark circles on template plastic: one with a radius of 2¼ inches for B, and one with a radius of 2 inches for C. Cut out these shapes to make templates.

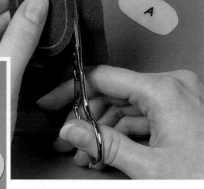

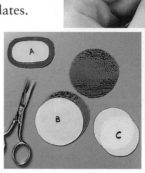

Trace template A onto the wrong side of a scrap of dark fabric. **Cut out the fabric, adding a scant ¼-inch seam allowance.** Trace two B circles on medium fabric and one C circle on a light fabric. **Cut the circles out along the marked lines.**

4

Tip

To make a dogwood blossom, use four pinched yo-yos, and cluster French knots at the center.

With each B and C piece, **make a raw-edge yo-yo.** Begin with a knot, and hand sew a running stitch approximately ⅛ inch from the raw edge all around the circle. Pull the thread to gather the edges tightly together and form a smaller circle, with the right side of the fabric out. Do not cut the thread; instead, bring it over the edge of the yo-yo, and back through the yo-yo center. Pull the thread to pinch one edge, and back-stitch at the yo-yo center on the gathered side to secure. Use the smooth side for the pansy petal.

5

Tip

Look at pansies in books or garden centers for realistic color combinations. Use velveteen or silk to simulate the texture of the real thing.

Appliqué the petals to the background along the top half of each shape. Start with shape A at the top center. Turn the seam allowance under and appliqué the top edge. Position the B petals so they meet at the center and cover the bottom of piece A. Imagine the pansy as a clock-face. Place the pinched areas of one B at 8 o'clock and the other at 4. Appliqué the top edges. Position piece C over the two B pieces, with the pinch at 6 o'clock; appliqué the top edge only. **Using embroidery floss, stitch yellow and black lines radiating out from the center.**

Peony

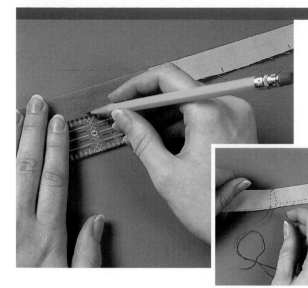

Cut a 1½ × 6½-inch strip of light pink fabric and a 1½ × 8½-inch strip from both a medium and dark pink fabric. Sew the strips together end to end. Fold the strip lengthwise, right sides out, and press. **Measuring from the seams, mark one raw edge at 2-inch intervals.** Begin at the light end. **Use a running stitch to sew diagonal lines that create a V.** Loop the thread over the folded end at the point of the V. Then sew ⅛ inch from the long raw edge to the first mark, sew a V, and repeat for the third mark.

Tip

Press the seams open and trim them to reduce bulk.

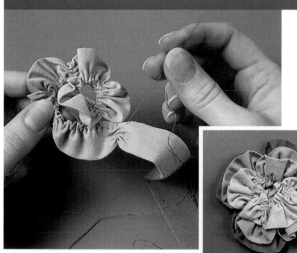

Pull the thread gently to gather the fabric, creating two petals. Backstitch to secure. **Continue stitching, gathering, and securing after every two or three Vs to form one or two petals at a time.** Tightly gather the first six petals and loosely gather subsequent petals. **After the strip is completely gathered, arrange the spirals into three rounds or coils, with the lightest petals on top.** Secure the rounds in place with tacking stitches on the back.

Tip

By gathering and knotting after each pair of petals, you'll limit the restitching needed if the thread should break.

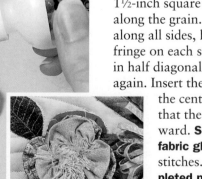

To make the peony center, cut a 1½-inch square of yellow fabric along the grain. Pick out the threads along all sides, leaving ¼ to ½ inch of fringe on each side. Fold the square in half diagonally, and then in half again. Insert the pointed center into the center of the flower, so that the fringe extends outward. **Secure with a dab of fabric glue** or a few tacking stitches. **Appliqué the completed peony flower to the background fabric,** stitching all around its outer edge.

A GARDEN OF FLOWERS

Daisy

1

Bond two different pieces of gold fabric together, as described in Step 2 on page 74. Cut a 2½ × 3-inch rectangle from this two-sided fabric. Fold in half lengthwise, with the fabric you'd like to show the most on the outside, and sew a running stitch along the raw edges opposite the fold. **Beginning about ⅛ inch from one short edge, cut into the fold at ⅛-inch intervals.** Be careful not to cut the basting stitches. **Pull the basting thread to gather the piece tightly;** stitch to connect the ends.

2

To make the daisy center, cut a fabric circle 1¼ inches in diameter. Sew a running stitch ⅛ inch from the edge all around the circle; do not cut the thread. Roll a 1¼-inch square of batting into a ball, and place it on the wrong side of the fabric circle. **Pull the thread ends to gather the circle tightly around the ball of batting,** and secure the ball with a knot. Tack the daisy flower to the background fabric catching the bottom layer of petals only. Appliqué the raised center in place.

Variegated Rose

1

Use a ⅝-inch-wide wire-edge ribbon shaded light to dark in one color family. Cut an 18-inch piece, fold it in half crosswise, and crease the midpoint. Pull the wire along the lighter edge up to this crease, gathering half the length of ribbon. **Then, from the opposite end, pull the wire along the darker edge** to gather the rest of the ribbon. Coil the ribbon, beginning with the gathered light end face up and **flipping to the darker color at the midpoint.**

Tip

For more ideas on using synthetic florals, see "Velvet Leaves & Silk Flowers" on page 68.

Secure the rose petals in place with tacking stitches on the back. **Manipulate the wire edges to curve the petals, and curl the edges in.** Use matching-color thread to appliqué the rose to the background fabric. For leaves, cut motifs from floral prints or use velvety, synthetic rose leaves cut from silk flower stems or purchased in packages.

A Floral Bouquet

If you like, you can arrange various flowers into a bouquet on a background, add a dimensional bow, and **showcase the design inside a round or oval window opening** that works like a mat on a picture. Use a thin line of fabric glue to adhere lace trim along the edge of the opening, and when the glue is dry, blindstitch the lace edges (or topstitch them by machine) to secure the trim in place.

Actual-Size Patterns

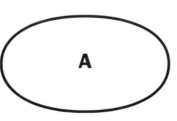

A

**Scottish
Thistle Leaf**

Pansy Flower Top Petal A

Daisy Leaf

It's a fact that most of our quilts are made with love, no matter why we make them or for whom. There are special quilts, however, that also aim to tell a story—of a birth, marriage, anniversary, or birthday; of a once-in-a-lifetime journey; or of a life remembered. A successful story quilt brings together bits and pieces of memorabilia, and working with them can present quite a challenge! Have no fear: This chapter provides not only inspiration for what embellishments to include, but also the nuts and bolts on how to include them.

Getting Started

The special occasion or honoree will help determine the items you select for your memory quilt. Consider what you'd most like to recognize about that person or event, and the mood you wish to convey, be it romantic, humorous, or elegant. Don't worry if your initial search yields too much memorabilia. Variety increases your options, allowing you to select the embellishments that tell your story best. Gather all the odds and ends, and let the mixture "percolate" in your imagination.

You can use many different settings as the backdrop for your memory quilt. You might incorporate your memorabilia into traditional pieced or appliquéd blocks, using each block to tell a "chapter" of the story, or feature key items in a medallion-style arrangement. Use a design wall to audition several arrangements before you make a final decision, and take pictures or outline rough sketches on graph paper for easy reference. There are few, if any, rules here. If you've never designed a quilt before, this is a great opportunity to experiment and stretch your creativity.

What You'll Need

Fabrics for background

Variety of memorabilia

Velcro, snaps, hooks, and other temporary fasteners

Decorative threads, ribbons, and yarns

Photos and other printed matter

Heat-sensitive transfer paper

Ink Jet or Bubble Jet Inkset

Tightly woven pima cotton for photo transfers

Iron and ironing surface

Small sheets of clear vinyl

Tissue paper

Telling Someone's Story

Apparel & Accessories

Small articles of clothing or personal accessories nicely chronicle a person or event in your memory quilt. Gloves, handkerchiefs, small evening bags, tiny satin baby shoes, booties, bonnets, scouting patches, emblems, varsity letters, and even bridal lace can be attached to a quilt with tacking or decorative stitches. Larger or heavier items, such as leather gloves or a vintage christening dress, are more of a challenge. For a simple solution, try snaps, buttons, or dots of Velcro.

Tip

Use temporary fasteners for items or garments you prefer to remove when laundering or storing a quilt.

Honoring Handwork

Is your quilt a tribute to someone who produced needlework such as knitting, crewel, embroidery, cross-stitch, redwork, tatting, or lace? Was this person a quilter who left behind orphan quilt blocks? **Small pieces of handwork may be tacked or appliquéd to the quilt surface**, setting the tone and the color scheme for the quilt design. They may also be used as the focal point or pieced into the quilt's background—an especially nice touch if the original handwork was signed by the honoree.

Significant Pins & Jewelry

Especially meaningful or symbolic items, such as **fraternity or antique hat pins; tie tacks; pin-on name tags; military medals; cameos, brooches, and other vintage jewelry, do triple duty by decorating the surface, advancing the story, *and* helping to anchor other embellishments.** You might also include religious medallions or other mementoes, such as ribbons from competitions.

Pouches or Pockets

To show off ticket stubs, postcards, coins, or other small souvenirs, encase them in clear vinyl. Cut the vinyl to the appropriate size. Thread your machine with contrasting-color thread, set it for a zigzag or other simple, decorative stitch, and insert a new needle (16/100). Position the vinyl shapes and items as desired. Pin a larger piece of tissue paper over the vinyl, placing the pins just outside the vinyl's edge. (The vinyl won't have pinholes, and the tissue will allow the presser foot to move easily.) Stitch, then **remove the tissue paper,** using tweezers to remove smaller bits.

Transferring Photos to Fabric

It is easy to transfer photographic images to fabric; use heat-sensitive transfer paper, a color copier, a piece of tightly woven cotton fabric, and a hot, dry iron. You can follow instructions on the transfer paper to do this at home, or visit a copy shop for assistance. Select fabric with a high thread count, such as pima cotton, for the clearest image, and carefully follow any directions regarding pressing the finished image. **Be aware that your transferred image will be the reverse of your original.**

Tip

For a finished image that's an exact duplicate of the original, ask your copy center to reverse the photocopy.

Transferring Printed Material

To get printed words on your quilt, use inkset, a solution that makes fabric more receptive to printer inks. Saturate a fat quarter with inkset, and hang the fabric to dry until it's stiff. Iron the wrong side of the fabric to the shiny side of freezer paper. Cut the fabric and paper to fit your printer or copier. **Insert it and print text right from your computer, or photocopy it.** Let the fabric sit for a day, rinse with cold water, and remove the freezer paper. **Use portions of your fabric print as appliqués or patches in your quilt.**

Tip

While pima cotton gives the clearest prints, you may prefer muslin for a nostalgic, faded look.

Spell It Out

There are several other ways to add lettering to your quilt. **Announce the name and vital statistics of a newborn in stenciled lettering.** (Let the fabric paint stand on its own or serve as a pattern for satin-stitch embroidery.) You could also stitch letters by hand, use a programmable sewing machine, or use free-motion stitching to write in cursive. Include phrases from that special song for the bridal or anniversary couple, or use red, white, and blue alphabet buttons to spell out key dates and places for the military veteran.

MEMORY MAKERS

Framing Devices

Tip

Cut little black triangles from fusible-backed fabric to simulate old-fashioned photo album corners.

Spotlight transferred photographs, invitations, and other mementos by "framing" them with decorative foils and trims. **Tack beads over vintage lace.** Couch or work embroidery over wide grosgrain ribbon, braid, or other decorative trims to give the photo transfers added importance and a fine, finished appearance.

For a more realistic-looking frame, fuse gold or silver fabric foil or lamé to the background, then appliqué, topstitch, or fuse the transfer in place.

Home Sweet Home

Tip

Use pintucks to replicate clapboard, quilting to provide the mortar around bricks, and blanket stitch by machine to create staggered rows of shingles.

Call on all your embellishment skills to render a house in fabric. Start from a photo or sketch, enlarging it on a photocopier, if necessary. Use lace trims for gingerbread molding, beads for doorknobs, or embroidery for fine linear details. Landscape your house with a flower garden of silk ribbon embroidery and threadpainted shrubbery. Create dimensional fir trees using two bonded pieces of fabric. Just cut boughs of graduating sizes, and fringe the bottom edges. Then stitch along the top edges to secure, and let the fringe hang free.

The AIDS Memorial Quilt

Tip

If you wish to make a panel for a friend or loved one, contact the Names Project Foundation for more information; see "Resources" on page 126.

The AIDS Memorial Quilt is the ultimate memory quilt, started in 1987 and still under construction today. Contributors all share the common desire to remember a loved one who died of AIDS. Each contributor makes a 3 × 6-foot bound panel. Panels are displayed in public places, in small groups, or **in giant arrangements with just enough space between them so people can inspect them closely.**

Panels document the name and hometown of the deceased, and often dates of birth and death, in stitching, textile paint, stenciling, or fabric markers. Photo transfers are encouraged.

MEMORY MAKERS

Making Memories That Hang Straight

Problem	Solution
Your quilt doesn't hang properly with the added (and varying) weight of your memorabilia.	An important consideration in the final design is balance, both literally and figuratively. A memory quilt will most likely be displayed on a wall, so you'll want it to be squared-up and free of wavy edges. ❑ If possible, redistribute heavier embellishments more evenly over the surface of the quilt, or move them toward the bottom so the finished piece is "weighted" and hangs nicely. ❑ Stitch drapery weights along the bottom edge, just above the binding, on the back of your quilt. As an alternative, sew a sleeve to the bottom as well as to the top edge of the quilt, and insert a strip of lattice to straighten the edge and add weight. ❑ Quilt heavily in the background. Close quilting such as stippling in the background draws the quilt top close to the batting and backing. The embellishments are less likely to sag. In addition, the meandering stitches draw diverse embellishments together and add texture and interest. For added sparkle, use variegated or metallic threads.

Customize your quilt backgrounds.

Use photo transfers to create unique fabric for the background of your memory quilt. For example, transfer old love letters, wedding and birth announcements, and sheet music of your parent's "special song" to pima cotton and piece these fabrics as a backdrop for their 50th anniversary remembrance quilt.

Use stenciling or rubber stamping to transform muslin, subtle prints, or solids into custom fabric for your memory quilts, or adapt commercial fabrics with paint or fabric markers. For instance, a fabric with appropriate flowers can be colored to match the bridal bouquet.

Try This!

Incorporate nostalgia into any quilt.

Memorabilia can play a starring role in a memory quilt, and it can provide special meaning in traditional quilts, too. Use Grandma's vintage lace to trim the edges of traditional Grandmother's Fan blocks, or use seashells collected from family outings to highlight a Sailboat quilt for your favorite weekend sailor. Place a few carefully chosen photos of your family and pets in the doors and windows of your favorite House blocks or in the centers of Attic Windows blocks.

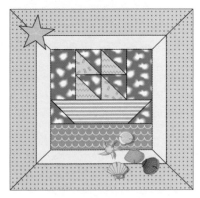

MEMORY MAKERS

Under the Sea:
Atmospheric Effects

Nature provides endless sources of inspiration for quilters and all artists. Perhaps a snorkeling adventure left you dreaming of creating an underwater fantasy in fabric. Maybe you want to capture a breathtaking scene glimpsed through early morning fog. Here's good news: You can transfer all that color, texture, and atmosphere to your quilts with thread, paint, yarn, and translucent fabrics. Read on to discover how to threadpaint exotic fish or other creatures, add gauze for swaying seaweed or wild grasses, stamp bubbles, or add an overlay of shimmering mist. You'll create a naturalist's paradise right in your sewing room.

Getting Ready

Creating a mood with fabric, thread, and other embellishments can be an exciting experience. If you're artistically inclined, try sketching an original scene to use as a guide for making your quilt. If you prefer to work from a photo or graphic illustration, look through magazines, postcards, photography books, art books, posters, and even children's books for inspiration. Once you've settled on a design, assemble various fabrics, colors, and textures that fit the quilt's mood and theme. Include a theme-appropriate background fabric or a tightly woven, solid-color cotton. Collect transparent fabrics such as cheesecloth, gauze, organza, and netting. Then take an inventory of your thread collection and add to it—the more varieties and color options you have, the better. For many of the effects described in this chapter, 30-weight rayon makes an excellent choice, but also consider threads such as Madeira Supertwist, Sulky Sliver, and various neon, metallic, and variegated threads. Use a cotton thread in the bobbin.

What You'll Need

Tightly woven, solid-color cotton fabrics

A variety of gauzy and sheer novelty fabrics

Light box

Sulky Totally Stable

Black fine-tip marker

Sewing machine with darning foot

A variety of decorative threads, yarns, and trims

Light- and medium-weight threads in assorted colors

Machine-embroidery hoop

Medium-weight iron-on fusible web

Iron, press cloth, and ironing surface

Fabric paint

Tailor's awl or stiletto

Threadpainted Appliqués

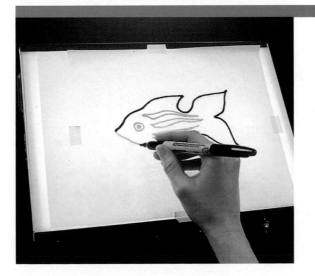

A threadpainted appliqué depicting a recognizable animal, plant, or object can be a wonderful focal point to set off less-realistic effects. If this is your first experience with free-motion threadpainting, start with a simple design. Enlarge or reduce it as desired, and place it design side down on a light box so you can trace the reverse image. (Your finished appliqué will then match the original design.) Place a piece of Sulky Totally Stable iron-on fabric stabilizer on top, matte side up, and **use a black fine-tip marker to transfer your design.**

Tip

A mottled, hand-dyed fabric makes a great background for a design that will not be totally covered with threadpainting.

2

Next, select a tightly woven background fabric in the predominant color of your appliqué, in case you wish to cover only part of the background with threadpainting or the background shows through your stitches. Cut the fabric large enough to fit in your hoop. Place the stabilizer, shiny side down, on top of the wrong side of your fabric. **Iron the stabilizer to the fabric.**

Tip

Don't worry if you haven't mastered free-motion stitchery: These outlines will all be covered.

3

Lower the feed dogs of your sewing machine, and use a darning foot and a 90/14 needle. Free-motion stitch along the drawn lines. **Use a top thread that will contrast with the lines, like red thread over black lines,** so you can easily see which lines you have followed and which you have yet to go over. Use a thread in the bobbin that will contrast clearly with the background fabric you've chosen, so **when you flip your work over to the right side, you'll have a clear, outlined image.**

4

Stretch the image, fabric side up, in a machine embroidery hoop. Use an appropriate-color rayon thread and a similarly colored cotton thread in the bobbin. With the feed dogs still lowered and using a zigzag stitch, start with a few tiny stitches in place to secure. Then, **fill in an area with close, wide, overlapping zigzag stitches (satin stitch).** Maintain uniform directions that suit the design. End with a few tiny stitches, and leave thread tails. If these thread tails aren't buried by future stitches, you can trim them off later.

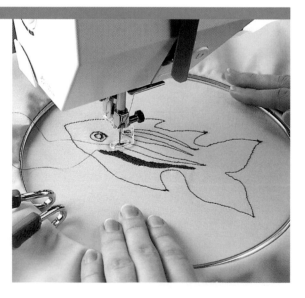

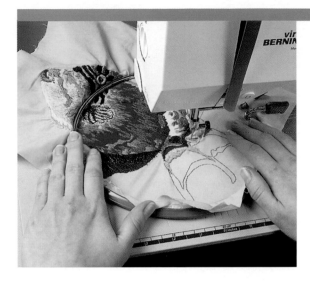

For a more complex design, you will want to change thread colors. Stagger your rows of stitches to make these changes gradual. To save time, work over thread ends. Also, try to work with one thread color at a time and do all the sections that you'll want in this color. To move to a different part of the motif, take a few tiny straight stitches, lift the needle, and "drag" the thread to the new area, then continue stitching.

Tip

Use progressive values of thread color (light to dark, or vice versa) for smooth transitions.

6

Use contrasting types of threads to create special effects. For example, **slick, decorative threads such as Sulky Sliver Metallics in black and opalescent give fish eyes the "wet look."**

Tip

Omit the hoop and hold the stabilized fabric taut with your hands to work near the edges of your design.

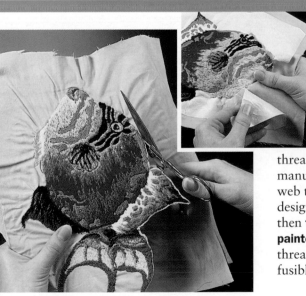

7

When the appliqué is totally covered with thread, remove it from the hoop, and **tear away the stabilizer around the threadpainted design.** Cut a piece of paper-backed fusible web a few inches larger than the threadpainted motif, and follow the manufacturer's directions to press the web to the wrong side of the stitched design. Allow the fusible web to cool, then **trim closely around the thread-painted appliqué;** avoid cutting any threads along the edges. Remove the fusible web's paper backing.

UNDER THE SEA: ATMOSPHERIC EFFECTS

8

Tip

Iron your
appliqué from
the back, as
well, to ensure
a good bond
with the quilt
top.

Position the appliqué on the quilt top, and use a hot, dry iron and a press cloth to fuse it in place. **Secure the appliqué to the quilt with the same free-motion, wide zigzag stitch you used for threadpainting.** Work with one color at a time, angling and matching the threadpainting so the stitches blend seamlessly into the edges of the original threadwork. Work over the entire raw edge of the motif, covering any remaining background fabric. It should look like you've done all of the stitching on the quilt itself, rather than on the individual appliqué.

More Special Effects

Instant Appliqués

Tip

Try some
other options:
Finish the raw
edges with a
satin stitch,
zigzag stitch,
or couching
with chenille
yarn or rayon
braid.

For an easy but effective appliqué shortcut, **select a few printed or batik fabrics featuring marine motifs, large leaves, florals, or other appropriate designs.** Look to other fabrics as well. That "fireworks" print might make an unexpectedly *perfect* coral! Apply fusible web to the back of each fabric, centering it over the motif you wish to feature. Cut out the images, play with their arrangement, and then **fuse them to the quilt.** For added security, topstitch along the raw edges.

Images with Gauze

Tip

Use an appli-
qué pressing
sheet to
protect your
iron from
any melted
adhesive
coming
through the
gauze.

To add texture and translucence, try a loosely woven fabric such as cheesecloth or gauze. Hand-dye large pieces, **letting colors blend together.** Trace or draw images on the paper backing of fusible web. Since the web will be fused to the back of the fabric, the final image will be reversed. Follow the manufacturer's directions to **adhere the web to the gauze.** Remove the backing, fuse the element to your quilt, and topstitch the edges of the gauze to secure it.

Sheer Atmosphere

Create more ethereal effects by overlaying all or part of your design with fusible appliqués of see-through fabric such as tulle, organza, chiffon, or netting. Apply fusible web in the same way as gauze or cheesecloth. Mark circular bubbles or slender, curving stalks on the paper backing. **Cut out these shapes along the marked lines,** peel away the paper, arrange the shapes on the quilt top, and fuse them in place. Secure these motifs with free-motion topstitching as well.

Stamping

The ends of plastic spools make wonderful stamps for perfectly round bubbles. Look for sparkly or glossy varieties of fabric paints such as StarBright, by Jacquard. Dip the spool in the paint and then stamp directly on the quilt top. Twist the spool around in position to distribute the paint in a complete circle. You can dip the spool again and position it in the same place for a heavier paint outline. Globs or spatters will enhance the bubble effect, and a dab of paint applied with a paintbrush can create a subtle glint on a bubble.

A Tangle of Yarns & Threads

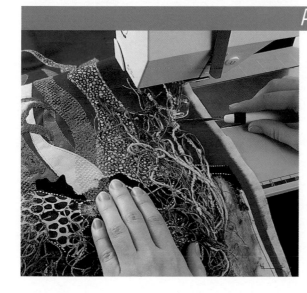

For under-the-sea scenes, slubby yarns and shiny or variegated threads can be combined to suggest seaweed swaying in the underwater currents. In other landscapes, earth-tone strands provide a fringe of weeds or wild grasses. With the feed dogs down, use a darning foot, a straight or zigzag stitch, and a matching or clear thread. Move slowly and in all directions to free-motion "tack" strands and clumps loosely in place. **Keep strands from getting tangled in the foot by flattening or moving them aside with a tailor's awl or stiletto.**

Tip

For extra texture, start with knotted fibers, or let some strands dangle freely.

UNDER THE SEA: ATMOSPHERIC EFFECTS

Puttin' on *the Glitz*

All that glitters isn't gold…it's also silver, bronze, metallic hues of every color, spangled, studded, bejeweled, and mirrored. Dramatic, shimmering quilts are nothing new. Many classic and timeless crazy quilts of the Victorian era literally glowed with an assortment of silken threads, shiny buttons, and glistening trims. Why not pair this Victorian pastime with today's wealth of dazzling materials—rhinestones, paints, foils, and lamé—to create an opulent ode to the new millennium?

Getting Ready

Whether your goal is lavish Victorian elegance, space-age dazzle, sophisticated glamour, or a cityscape at night, this is your chance to pull out all the stops. Collecting the various threads, trims, and trinkets is all part of the fun. Think of it as a giant treasure hunt! While many of the requisite treasures can be found in your local fabric shop or craft store, don't quit there. Explore estate and tag sales for inexpensive costume jewelry, secondhand stores for abandoned eveningwear (often loaded with "gems," sequins, spangles, and appliqués), home improvement centers for shiny metallic hardware, and party stores for glossy ribbons, streamers, glitter, tinsel, and sparkly confetti.

A word of advice: Read the labels and test all paints and adhesives on scraps of your fabrics before using them on one-of-a-kind creations. This will alert you to any potential problems or pitfalls, and you'll also be familiar with laundering details such as whether a project can be washed and whether or not to heat-set before washing.

What You'll Need

- **Lamé and shiny fabrics**
- **Variety of fabric paints, sticks, and markers**
- **Freezer paper**
- **Variety of paintbrushes and stencils**
- **Rhinestones and "jewels"**
- **Strong glue or epoxy**
- **Metal charms**
- **Cotton and decorative threads**
- **Glossy ribbons**
- **Sequins**
- **Patches and appliqués**
- **Decorative studs**
- **Pliers or screwdriver**
- **Shisha mirrors**
- **Metallic braids and trims**
- **Fusible interfacing**

Sources of Sparkle

Space-Age Gleam

You can transport even a traditional Mariner's Compass design to celestial heights with a little glitzy fabric. Lamé and other metallic fabrics are available at stores that sell garment-making fabrics. Look in end-of-bolt or remnant baskets for small pieces, or browse specialty fabric vendors at major quilt shows. Stabilizing these fabrics with lightweight, fusible interfacing makes them easier to cut and piece. Do not touch lamé with a hot iron, however; the metallic threads could melt instantly. Use a press cloth and press from the wrong side.

Add subtle sparkle with quilter's cottons that are printed with gold or silver highlights.

Easy Embroidered Elegance

Tip

A sharp, new Metafil needle will reduce your odds of experiencing thread-breakage and tension difficulties.

Familiar hand or machine embroidery stitches worked in metallic threads can lend a bit of sparkle. **Spirals of chain stitches in silver suggest whorls of icy wind or snow; simple cross-stitches become glistening snowflakes.** Hand-stitching lets you use heavy threads and isolated stitches to tie the quilt layers together while adding decoration. If you prefer to embellish by machine, it's easiest to do so before the quilt is basted. Select slick rayons, smooth foil-wrapped metallics, ribbonlike metallic films, or other exciting, shiny threads.

The Midas Touch

Tip

Create the look of a ruched flower by stitching loops and coils of metallic trims into blossom shapes.

Add a more substantial glow with fancy trims that feature a precious-metal finish. Insert metallic gold piping into seams or appliqué ribbon woven with gleaming threads over the corners of a block. Couch gold braid and passementerie trims in radiating or intersecting lines, or sew metallic lace and trims in place with decorative embroidery stitches. To attach, use gold thread to mimic the details of the trims, or use contrasting colors for variety.

Light Up the Dark

Tip

Avoid slick, puffy fabric paints: Applications can't be ironed or folded, and washings will dull paints and remove glitter.

Generate dramatic special effects with sparkling fabric paints. Use a smooth, tightly woven, dark-color background fabric to really set these paints off. Back the fabric with freezer paper, then apply metallic acrylic paints freehand on the stabilized surface. Experiment with applicator-tip bottles, oil paint sticks, and metallic fabric markers and pens. **For extra glitz, sprinkle on glitter while paints are still wet.** Use the fabrics as backgrounds, in piecework, or **cut out pieces to use as appliqués.**

P U T T I N ' O N T H E G L I T Z

Ready-Made Appliqués

If you long for something even more over the top, glamour-wise, but lack the time (or inclination) to create these detailed accents, **purchase embroidered patches and decorative appliqués. A guitar, musical note, treble clef, or star may be just the ticket for making your quilt rock and roll.** You'll find these clever timesavers in all kinds of motifs in the notions departments of most fabric stores. Some are iron-ons, but you'll probably want to sew them to your quilt for added security. Blindstitch them in place by hand, or machine-zigzag with clear monofilament or matching thread.

Glorious Jewels

Add sparkling detail to your quilts with a glittering variety of baubles, bangles, and beads. Look for sew-on jewels, rhinestones, and faceted crystal beads. For maximum impact, the bigger and glitzier, the better. If you can't find jewels to stitch in place, substitute glue-on jewels. **These no-fuss alternatives are easily secured with a dab of adhesive,** such as Gem Tack or Beacon Magna-Tac, made especially for attaching jewels to fabric.

Charmed, I'm Sure

Charms aren't just for bracelets anymore! **Select these gold or silver icons specifically to reflect the theme of your quilt or the interests of the person for whom you are making it.** Stores, catalogs, and websites for beading and jewelry-making supplies carry a huge variety of shiny or antiqued metal trinkets. Scatter or cluster them on your quilt after quilting, so they don't tangle your quilting stitches. For added elegance, attach them with shiny threads, glossy ribbons, or sparkly beads.

Tip

You can change the patina of a charm by painting it with a pearly, pastel nail polish.

PUTTIN' ON THE GLITZ

Twinkle, Twinkle

Tip

View your quilt
in progress
from a dis-
tance, or
through a
reducing glass,
to be sure
glitzier
elements are
evenly
distributed.

Sequins and spangles reflect light like a disco ball. **You'll find them in many sizes and colors, and in flat, die-cut shapes such as snowflakes, stars, and daisies.** Holiday motifs are perfect for pictorial or theme quilts. Attach individual sequins with matching thread; secure them with tiny seed beads for even more shine. **Also, stitch strings of sequins and sequin-embellished metallic braid to your quilts.** These trims are perfect for decorating the seams of elaborate crazy quilts.

Nailheads & Studs

Tip

Give your
project added
stability by
backing light-
weight fabrics
with fusible
cotton inter-
facing before
adding studs or
nailheads.

Metallic nailheads and decorative studs are super sources of easy, no-sew shine! These embellishments are **available in a variety of shapes and colors.** Look for them in fabric and craft stores, and **use them to represent decorations, knobs, stars, or bubbles.** To attach a stud, position it on the quilt top as desired, and gently poke the prongs through to the back of the fabric. Turn the quilt top over; use pliers or a screwdriver to bend the prongs down and toward each other.

Say It with Shishas

Tip

Use this same
technique to
attach any
round, flat
object without
a hole, such as
a shiny coin or
token.

Reflective shisha mirrors, with their hint of Eastern mystery, add an exotic touch to a quilt's surface. Work over a surface stabilized with a foundation or interfacing. Temporarily secure the shisha with a glue stick (1), then use colorful pearl cotton thread to stitch over the mirror in a star-shaped grid (2,3). **Finish by working a buttonhole stitch all around the mirror's outer edge (4);** work over the framework of threads and pull stitches taut so as to reveal more of the mirror (5).

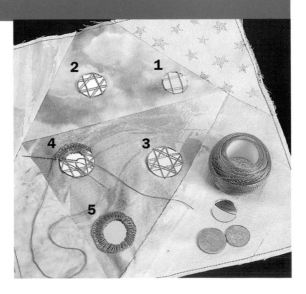

The Quilter's
Problem Solver

Avoiding Glitz Overkill

Problem	Solution
You want to add sparkly beads, sequins, metallic trims, and lamé to your quilt, but you're worried about overdoing it.	Strive for balance when working with highly reflective embellishments and fabrics. Use your design wall to preview the selection, placement, and quantity of these dramatic materials before attaching them to your quilt with thread or glue. Here are a few additional tips for keeping the end results tasteful rather than tacky. ❑ Assign glitz a supporting role, rather than the starring role. Use sparkly metallic threads for quilting, for stitching pintucks, or for couching other, nonmetallic threads, ribbons, or yarns. Think accent, no more. ❑ Even in the most glamorous quilt, include a wide range of different finishes in your final selection: some glittery and polished, others matte or with a subtle sheen. ❑ For an understated, tailored look, keep shiny embellishments, such as glass buttons and metallic beads, similar in color and value to the background fabrics. If you'd like a little more impact, introduce contrast, but concentrate on one or two color combinations, such as a color-wheel triad of violet, green, and orangey gold. ❑ Adopt a classic trick of fashion consultants: Layer on all the "jewelry" you think you'd like, then remove a piece!

Put on a fabric-fix-up workshop.

Involve your guild in a one-hour activity or have a play-day with some friends, so you can share rubber stamps, ink pads, and the cost of a few new items. Object: To use no-sew glitzy embellishments to spark up lifeless pieces of fabric. Start with unimposing solids or tone-on-tone prints. At one station, put out some of the new metallic ink pads and rubber stamps—or just artist's and pencil erasers. At another station, set out appropriate glue, small glittery rhinestones, multicolor sequin polka dots, and perhaps sequin waste to cut up. Visit one or both stations, and hone your skills for stamping or using special glues.

Try This!

Create art fabrics á la Jackson Pollock.

If you're feeling especially free-spirited, apply shiny metallic paints without a plan. First, be sure that both you and the surrounding area are well protected! Wear an old shirt and gloves, and work over a plastic tarp or drop cloth. Load a dry paintbrush with metallic fabric paint, then flick, drip, or splatter the paint randomly onto one fat quarter of fabric at a time. Dip an old toothbrush or bottlebrush into the paint, and run your fingers or a skewer through the bristles to mist fine dots of paint onto the fabric. Let it dry, heat set it with an iron, and cut the fabric into patches, appliqués, or any setting element you choose.

Directing *the Eye*

Bring on the special effects! Use embellishments such as luminous beads, textured threads, and sparkling foils to lead the viewer's eye where you want it to go. Take your quilt to the next level by incorporating eye-catching embellishments where they'll have the greatest impact. Spotlight the strong points of the fabrics and pattern; control the flow of design elements. Lights, cameras, action! It's all up to you.

Getting Ready

Before you add any embellishing highlights, survey your quilt to determine *where* you want to focus attention. Perhaps you have a fabulous ethnic or vintage textile you wish to enhance, or subtly gradated hand-dyed fabrics that call for added emphasis. Maybe it's a landscape searching for focus, a strippy-style quilt in need of extra "punch," or a shy but beautifully appliquéd flower that whispers "Hey, what about me?"

Many of the basic embellishing techniques described in previous chapters can be put to work for you here—beading, couching, embroidery—no matter what stage of the process you're at. With the exception of the prairie point "arrows," almost all of the ideas and techniques illustrated here can be worked on a quilt top, a basted and layered quilt, or even a project that is already at the quilting stage.

Clear your design wall and play with the beads, threads, trims, and trinkets you've collected. Experiment on the quilt until you find the mix that makes you say "Eureka!"

What You'll Need

- **Quilt top or quilt, ready for embellishment**
- **Variety of beads, buttons, and other found objects**
- **Beading thread, such as Nymo**
- **Long, thin beading needle**
- **Repositionable fusible web, such as Steam-A-Seam 2**
- **Fabric foil in various colors**
- **Iron and ironing surface**
- **Fabric scraps for prairie points**
- **Rotary-cutting equipment**
- **Sewing machine**
- **Walking and cording feet**
- **Seam ripper**
- **Removable fabric marker**

Follow the Light

Spotlight on Focal Points

Cluster embellishments densely to strengthen a focal point. Beads and sequins, with their rich variety of color and built-in sparkle, are ideal for emphasizing particular elements of a quilt's design. **A heavy concentration of glittery gold and yellow beads and sequins, set off by the complementary matte textures of pompoms and dimensional fabric, has an almost hypnotic power to pull the viewer's eye into the center of a sunflower.** See "Puttin' on the Glitz" on page 92 for other gleaming accents to incorporate.

DIRECTING THE EYE

Tip

Because of
their elongated
shape, bugle
beads can be
especially
effective at
reinforcing
directional
imagery.

Beads can also draw the viewer from a focal point to other, less-prominent areas of a quilt. **Densely bead around the focal point, and work outward, placing beads farther apart as you proceed.** Attach them in radiating lines or widening spirals, or even in a scattered arrangement. Straight or curved rows of beads can also emphasize a design line or lead the eye along a specific route. For example, clear seed and bugle beads tracing a stream in a landscape quilt will both catch and direct the viewer's eye.

Accent on Foil

1

The sparkle from fabric foil, available at many craft and fabric stores, can be used to emphasize the focal point of your quilt. Cut the desired shapes from a repositionable paper-backed fusible web, such as Steam-A-Seam 2. Shapes such as arrowheads, triangles, and strips *direct*, while stars, spirals, and other such shapes *focus* the eye on key areas of the quilt. **Follow the manufacturer's directions and position the shapes on the quilt, paper side up.** Rearrange them until you're satisfied with their placement. Use an iron to *lightly* press the shapes onto the quilt.

2

Tip

Use a Teflon
pressing sheet
to protect
"finished" foil
during future
pressing, or
simply work
around these
shapes.

Remove the protective paper from the fusible web, and cover it with a sheet of fabric foil, color side up. The foil is attached to a cellophane pressing sheet that protects your iron during the application process. **Press with a hot, dry iron, moving over the foil three or four times.** When the foil sheet has cooled, peel it off the fabric, **leaving foil on the desired shape.** If it doesn't adhere perfectly, press fresh areas of the same sheet to cover these spots. Try using more than one color, for variety.

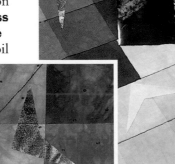

DIRECTING THE EYE

Other Dynamic Directionals

Prairie Point Arrows

Prairie points are ideal for directing the eye. Cut 4-inch fabric squares and **fold each square in half to form a rectangle. Bring the two corners of the folded edge to meet in the center, forming a triangle.** Pin the prairie points, folded side up, along various seam lines in a balanced arrangement, aiming the "tips" toward the focal point you wish to emphasize. **Open the seam and insert the long, raw edge of the prairie point.** Restitch the seam, and press.

For a touch of added sparkle, tack down the finished prairie points with clear or matching-color seed beads.

Walk the Line

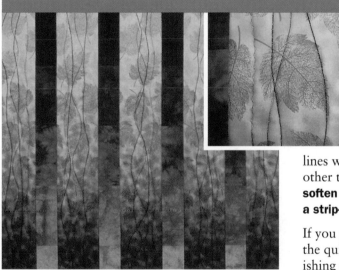

Lines of stitching worked in decorative threads and trims provide another means of directing the eye. Use a removable fabric marker to draw lines on your pieced or appliquéd quilt top. Couch over the lines with threads, yarns, ribbons, or other trims. **Graceful curves will soften the rigid, linear appearance of a strip-pieced art quilt.**

If you prefer, you can layer and baste the quilt first, so you'll be embellishing and quilting at the same time.

Try one of the various chalk markers to draw clear, easily removable couching lines.

Accents in a Row

Repeat eye-catching embellishments for visual emphasis. Just a few bold buttons, beads, shells, or other unique trinkets can lend importance to a design element deserving of a second look. **The three buttons beside the silk-screened foliage in this quilt balance the off-center motif, while the three different buttons below underscore the drama of this graphic piece of fabric.** In addition, when embellishments are spaced in a row as these are, the viewer's eye "connects" them to create a design line, or reinforce an existing one.

Add groups or clusters of embellishments in odd numbers (3, 5, and so on) for the most visually pleasing effect.

DIRECTING THE EYE

101

Embellishing
to the Rescue

It has happened to all of us at one time or another. That once-promising quilt top has run out of gas—or off the road! Now what? Not to worry: A quilter with a little courage and a toolbox of carefully chosen and well-placed embellishments can overcome just about any roadblock. So before you call Quilters' 911, try a few of these creative repairs. They're so effective, you'll want to use them even when a routine inspection of your quilt turns up no problems at all!

Getting Ready

There are many reasons why a quilt might need rescuing. Perhaps a fabric behaved disappointingly, your workmanship was less than ideal, or you simply lost interest in (or outgrew) the pattern or color scheme. Maybe the project was made for a challenge that imposed parameters you now wish to escape.

Place your quilt on a design wall or other flat surface so you can assess where embellishment might camouflage flaws or strengthen obvious weaknesses in design. Pin possible trims, threads, bead, buttons, and appliqués onto the quilt and view them from a distance. If you wish, record the various options with a Polaroid camera. Make notes, indicating the types and amounts of trims and embellishments you'll need.

Decide at what stage you'll make the improvements to your quilt. If you plan to embellish after layering and basting, use a busy print for the backing so the resulting stitching is less noticeable, and stabilize the quilt first by quilting the seam lines.

Creative Solutions

Wrinkle Repair

What do you do when one of your quilt fabrics, like a lamé that can't be ironed, has obvious crease marks? How do you add punch to a so-so quilt? Couching with decorative threads is the answer to both these questions. **Use it to cover up or camouflage creases, wrinkles, and puckers,** or to add movement to an otherwise static design by introducing strong diagonals or emphasizing eye-catching quilting motifs. See "Put Couching in Your Lineup" on page 14 for guidance.

Spice Up Your Strips

Tip

For a different look, stitch down the center of the trim, leaving the edges free. Or secure the trim with free-motion loops and curves.

Sometimes sashing strips, pieced panels, or borders can be overpowering in scale or color. Or maybe they're just too dull. Tone them down or spruce them up by **stitching a length of hand-dyed rayon tape, ribbon, or other flat trim right down the center.** Choose soft, subtle, or neutral shades for camouflage and bright, bold, or colorful hues to catch the eye. Select the width of the trim by determining how much of the original fabric you want to reveal. Secure both sides of the trim with a straight, zigzag, satin, or other decorative stitch.

Minor Mistakes

Tip

Disguise imperfect points and finish your quilt at the same time! Tie it at the troublesome seam intersections, using colorful floss, thread, or ribbon.

Oops! You've accidentally snipped a hole in your quilt top, pricked your finger and left a bloodstain, spilled a bit of coffee, or made a mark that won't wash out. **Or perhaps you've settled for some less-than-perfect piecing,** and now those mismatched points are all too noticeable. **Cover small holes or flaws with buttons or beads.** If chosen thoughtfully, these embellishments will appear well planned. Make sure to use the embellishment more than once, though, so it won't *look* like a cover-up.

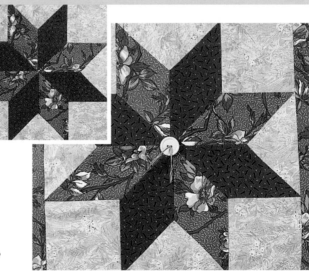

Major Flaws

Tip

Speed up your rescue mission with raw-edge appliqué or appliqués cut from synthetic suede, which does not ravel.

If the problem is over a larger area, a mere bead or button probably won't do the trick. You'll need a bigger cover-up. **Consider covering one or more major flaws with an appliqué motif in a complementary color or fabric,** or in a related theme. Audition various motifs, as well as various placements for the appliqués. You may find that instead of masking weaknesses, you prefer to place the appliqués where they simply draw attention away from areas you wish to de-emphasize.

Changing Color & Texture

Sometimes a fabric you used in your quilt disappoints you. Free-motion stitching can camouflage, cover, or just subtly alter the fabric, especially for a prominent appliqué piece. The colors and sheen of your thread and the lines or patterns of your stitches can give the entire quilt a different look. **Free-motion stitch over appliqués to pump up a weak color or to tone down an overpowering fabric.**

Tip

Appliqué sheer overlays of chiffon, tulle, or lace to tone down overpowering areas of your quilt top.

Lackluster Patches

Sometimes a fabric that looks perfect on the shelf doesn't hold its own when sewn into a quilt. **In this Churn Dash block, one of the triangle patches is too pale for the rest of the blues.** The good news: Even if the quilt is already completely assembled, you can still alter the fabrics. Brush a translucent fabric dye over the weak area, or **use markers to add curves or striations that will kick the fabric's appeal up a notch.**

Artful Disguises

Try to approach weak areas of a design as an artist. Use translucent fabric paints to apply a wash of color to an off-putting white space. Introduce pattern to a solid fabric by using fabric markers and a ruler to draw a few parallel or crosshatched lines, or any other subtle striations in one or more directions. Use a rubber stamp **or even the eraser end of a pencil dipped in fabric paint to add simple patterns to an overly quiet spot.** These and other paint techniques may also be used to mask a piece of fabric that is too busy or too loud.

Tip

Turn to "Stamps of Approval" on page 50 for rubber stamp how-tos.

EMBELLISHING TO THE RESCUE

Extraordinary *Sashings*

Sashing presents yet another opportunity to enhance your quilt with embellishment—and oh, the possibilities! Some options, such as playful peek-a-boo sashing, reflect a quiet, gentle personality, simply hinting at surprises to come. Others feature topstitched or inserted braids and trims, chunky rickracks, and gaily twisted ribbons that announce "Here I am!" with obvious decorative flair. Whether it's subtlety or sizzle, here are some fresh ideas to get those creative juices flowing!

Getting Ready

Are you listening? Your quilt is speaking to you, and the subject is sashing. Spread out your finished blocks because, as a group, they have a lot to say! When viewed together, your blocks reveal their color and design direction, telling you what they need to be connected as a "family." Do you hear a request for more color or a touch of quiet elegance? A shot of extra pizzazz, or just a little nudge? Gather threads, braids, and trims. Raid your button box and bead collection, and browse the aisles of your favorite quilt or sewing shop for interesting eyelets, ribbons, and lace.

Our suggestions embrace both hand and machine methods. Even if your quilt blocks are already assembled, there's something in this chapter for you. So take a moment to find those hand embroidery, tapestry, and chenille needles, *or* sit down and oil up your sewing machine.

What You'll Need

Quilt blocks or assembled quilt top

Rotary-cutting equipment

Thin batting such as low-loft polyester, cotton, or quilter's fleece

Sewing, embroidery, and other specialty needles

A variety of cotton and decorative threads

Sewing machine

Fabric and embroidery scissors

A variety of ribbons, braids, rickrack, and other trims

Buttons, ribbon rosettes, and other embellishments

Pins

Iron and ironing surface

Peek-a-Boo Sashing

Peek-a-boo (or inverted) sashing fools the eye; at first glance, there appears to be no sashing at all. **With a second look, a glimpse of color peeks out between the blocks.** For this technique, you'll need a set of blocks ready to be assembled into a quilt top. Decide on the color and fabric: Do you want your "peeks" to be spicy or subtle? Cut sashing strips to the desired width. One-third the finished width of the block is wide enough to accommodate a generous inverted pleat but not so wide that the pleat falls open too far. Cut the sashing lengths as usual.

Tip

If your quilt is made up of all solid fabrics, consider a print for the peek-a-boo sashing.

EXTRAORDINARY SASHINGS

2

Layer finished-size squares of thin batting behind each block and zigzag-stitch the batting in place around the block. Assemble the blocks and sashing strips. Beginning with a vertical sash, **fold the seamed edges so that two neighboring blocks meet in the center to form an inverted pleat.** Pin to secure. Hand tack at block intersections and press the pleat. Repeat for all remaining vertical sashes, then do the same for the horizontal sashing, **bringing pressed edges together to form intersections.**

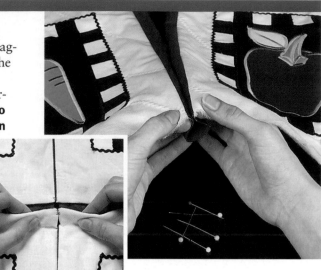

3

Add the borders. Layer and baste the quilt with your preferred batting (in addition to the batting basted to the blocks) and backing. Then secure the previously stitched intersections by hand or machine tacking through all three layers. Secure the intersections well, since these stitches tie your quilt together. If you like, **incorporate buttons into the new tacking stitches.** Other options are hand or machine embroidering with decorative threads and interesting stitches; catching ribbons or yarn in the stitches to make knots or bows; or adding beads or ribbon rosettes as you tack.

More to Consider

Ribbons, Braids & Trims

Tip

No sashing in your set? Use ribbon or trim to create a faux lattice.

Simply wonderful: Place a strip of special ribbon, passementerie braid, or other decorative trim down the center of each sashing strip. Use the same trim throughout, or mix and match. **Secure the trim with a fancy, decorative stitch worked in metallic or shiny rayon thread.** If your quilt design includes sashing squares, attach the trim before blocks and sashes are assembled; otherwise, attach it after assembly but before adding borders. This way, the raw ends of the trim will be hidden in the seams.

Twisted Ribbon

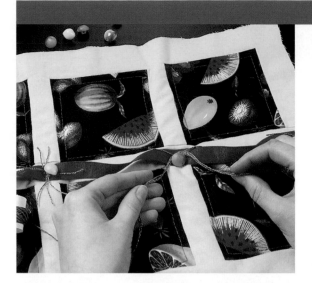

Here's a fun and easy way to use ribbon in your quilt. Before adding binding, pin a length of double-sided ribbon, grosgrain or satin, over each interior vertical or horizontal row of sashing, twisting the ribbon at the center of each block. Hand- or machine-tack the ribbon to your quilt, working at the intersections of sashing strips or more frequent intervals. Then hand-tack with a contrasting-color thread, such as pearl cotton. **Catch buttons in the tacking stitches, and then wrap the button with several more strands of the same thread.** Bind the quilt.

Rickrack

Rickrack adds a crisp charm to sashing. **Insert it in the seam when joining the block and sashing strip for a sawtooth finish.** Machine baste the rickrack around the edges of the block and sew just to the inside of these basting stitches when joining blocks.

For a bolder effect, attach rickrack directly over the seam with decorative stitching and colorful beads or tiny buttons. Or, **interlock two contrasting colors of rickrack to form a cable effect.** Sew this newly created trim down the center of each sashing strip.

Tip

Insert lace, eyelet trim, piping, ribbon folded in half lengthwise, or another trim into the seams between blocks and sashing.

Embellished Sashing Fabric

Create your own yardage for sashing strips. Couching, decorative machine stitchery, rubber stamping, painting, tie-dyeing, and pintucking are just some of the quick methods you can use to create your own distinctive fabrics. Make more than you'll need, **then use your rotary-cutting tools to cut sashing strips of the desired length and width.**

EXTRAORDINARY SASHINGS

Taking Trims
to the Edge

While traditional border and binding treatments can be effective and appropriate, sometimes a quilting project calls for something a little more "cutting edge." Buttons or grommets, prairie points, fringes of beads, yarn, fabric strips, or ribbon can all serve to add pizzazz on one, two, three, or four sides of your quilt. Whether your tastes favor homespun patchworks or jazzy, high-tech art quilts, you'll surely find the inspiration here for finishing your next quilt with flair!

Getting Ready

Take stock of where the quilt or quilted project is going to go. See the cautions in the "Where" section in "The 5 Ws of Embellishment," on page 12. Think about how extending the edges of your project will affect the overhang of a table runner or bed covering, or if an edging added to a vest might show below your coat hem.

Choose your embellishing materials and techniques so that they enhance, rather than compete with or overwhelm, the quilt design. Consider the quilt's overall style, mood, or theme. Simple, more subtle embellishments, such as soft, cozy yarns, will probably be more at home on traditional quilts than dangling trinkets and glittery threads. The latter, however, may be just the ticket for more contemporary designs.

Also, make sure that your selected embellishments are well-suited in scale and color to the rest of your project. Large, showy buttons may overpower the edges of a small wallhanging, while clear, tiny seed beads may be lost on the fringe of a full-size quilt.

What You'll Need

Quilted project ready for finishing

Variety of decorative threads, trims, and ribbons

Sewing machine

Cotton sewing thread

Variety of embellishments, such as beads, buttons, trinkets, and charms

Optional:

> **Beading thread such as Nymo or Silamide**
>
> **Hand-beading needles**
>
> **Rotary-cutting equipment**
>
> **Tailor's awl**
>
> **Small crochet hook**
>
> **Grommet kit**

Fabulous Finishes

Oversize Trim

For a simple but effective accent, stitch a bold decorative trim such as jumbo rickrack all around the edges of your quilt. Either "float" the trim over a wide border or cover the seam that joins the border or binding to the quilt. You can also use tassel or pompom trim, or wide grosgrain ribbon. Go a step beyond and layer on texture at the same time you secure the trim in place: Couch a high-contrast, decorative thread or narrower ribbon on top. For a more subtle look, insert rickrack, cording, folded grosgrain, or picot-edge ribbon into the binding seam.

Button Up!

Tip

If your quilt is destined for a bed, stick to flat buttons for comfort. For wall quilts, anything goes!

Add lots of additional color and texture by **attaching buttons, either at regular intervals or randomly spaced,** along the outer border, the binding, or the seam that joins the binding to your quilt. Choose buttons that reflect the quilt's mood or theme. Brightly colored, unusually shaped buttons project contemporary flair, while neutral-color, pearl, or wooden buttons inject a more homespun flavor.

See "Bring on the Buttons!" on page 20 for additional ideas on selecting buttons or making your own.

Beaded Fringe

Tip

Quicker and easier: Hang a beaded tassel from each corner of your quilt.

Beaded fringe makes a unique finishing touch for many quilted projects, such as wall hangings, table runners, and miniatures. Use a long, thin beading needle and thread it with a strong, neutral-color nylon thread made especially for beadwork, such as Nymo or Silamide. Refer to "The Basics of Beading" on page 26, for directions on dangling beads. For a polished look, place a small bead at the end of each strand of fringe. Be sure to secure the beginning and end of each strand of beads, so that if one strand falls apart, you won't lose a whole fringed edge.

Rag-Strip Fringe

Tip

For a more luxuriant-looking fringe, space lark's head knots more closely together.

For another fringe alternative, use one or more of the fabrics from your quilt (a great use for all of those cut-off selvage strips!) to make the classic macramé lark's head knot. Rotary-cut ½ × 12-inch strips. Use a tailor's awl to punch evenly spaced holes along the edge of your quilt, just beyond the binding. Insert a small crochet hook into a hole, **hook the center of a fabric strip, and bring up a loop.** Set aside the crochet hook and insert the ends of the strip through the loop. Pull the strip ends to **create a neat, tight knot.**

Ribbon Fringe

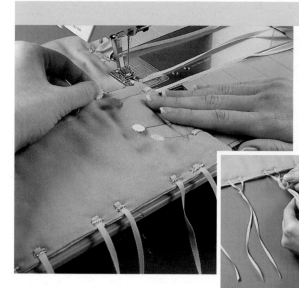

Ribbons are another fringing option. To attach the fringe, **fold one end of the ribbon over to form a ¼-inch hem, and secure it to the finished edge of the quilt with a decorative topstitch, such as the satin stitch.** Leave space between the strands, overlap them, or layer them, depending upon the look you prefer. For an even funkier finish, select a thread of contrasting color or texture, such as a sparkly metallic. Space these ribbons at regular intervals, or **space and tie them together in pairs.**

Tip

String a large decorative bead onto each knotted pair of ribbons, and finish with a second double knot.

Go High-Tech

Follow the directions that come with a grommet attachment kit (available in many sewing, craft, and home-decor shops) **to attach metal grommets along the borders or binding.** Grommets come in all sizes and colors. For a contemporary look, attach grommets at regular intervals or in groupings and leave them empty. Or, **tie strips of fabric, ribbon, or yarn through them.**

Tip

Consider colorful buttonholes—with or without openings or buttons—in place of grommets.

Dress Up Prairie Points

Prairie points add a wonderful touch to the edges of a quilt. Dress them up even more **by introducing patterns with decorative machine stitching or by dangling beads, buttons, charms, or other trinkets from the edges of each point.** Use strong floss or decorative thread to hand stitch embellishments in place.

You can also incorporate prairie points into your *borders*. Turn the points inward and catch them in the binding or outer border seam. **Use beads and threads to secure the points.**

Tip

Put tassels or pompoms at the ends of prairie points for a child's circus quilt or quilted valance.

A Bounty of Baskets

W e provided seven skilled embellishers with the same basic basket block, along with the instructions, "Embellish as you wish." The results? Incredibly varied...and simply fantastic! We couldn't help but feel inspired, and we think you will, too. So select a block and gather those buttons and beads, trinkets and trims, sequins and stamps, and set out to create your own embellished masterpiece!

Getting Ready

While this chapter concludes the book, it also provides many starting points for using the materials and methods described throughout to embellish your favorite traditional patterns. Pictorial blocks, such as the basket block used here, or others (such as houses, trees, or floral blocks) are naturals for embellishment, since they already suggest ways to "finish the picture." However, with just a little bit of experimentation, you'll soon discover that just about any block, from the most traditional to the most contempory, will serve as a canvas for artful embellishing.

To jump-start those artistic juices, read through this chapter to be inspired by our gallery of baskets. Then, turn to page 119, where you'll find diagrams of the basket block and a couple of other traditional blocks to photocopy, along with suggestions for creative play.

The Gallery

The Block as Star

Quilt artist and designer Elizabeth Rosenberg concentrated her efforts on embellishing the basket itself, forgoing the impulse to fill it. Elizabeth uses the geometric basket fabric to her advantage, echoing and enhancing the print design with luxurious couched trims and hand-stitched beads. A narrow band of glittering golden braid, accented along the top by ultra short, gold bugle beads, emphasizes the gracceful arc of the basket handle. The basket base provides a showcase for opulent, old-gold mesh ribbon, dramatically long bugle beads, and passementerie looped fringe along the top rim. This approach illustrates how you can dress up a traditional block, working with the fabric and using it as your inspiration for selecting simple, elegant embellishments.

Enhancing the Mood

Showing a delightful flair for the folk art look, instructor and author Alice Allen Kolb demonstrates her mastery of the sewing machine with a fanciful mix of color, texture, and patterning. Each embellishment and technique is carefully chosen to enhance the block's breezy country air. For "Sunday picnic" charm, Alice decided to have a "tablecloth" spilling out of the basket. It's a fusible appliqué that looks as if it had been inserted into the top seam of the basket, but it's actually satin-stitched in place all around, overlapping rickrack along the bottom edges. The flowers come alive with the aid of free-spirited, free-motion machine embroidery. Pearl cotton zigzag-stitched with the bobbinwork technique provides the heaviest design lines. Clusters of colorful seed beads plus a tiny black button, applied by hand, dot the flower centers; black seed beads provide texture along the basket bottom and handle.

Emulate a Favorite Era

A love of traditional 19th-century crazy quilts inspired this delicate Victorian fantasy. Teacher, author, and veteran embellisher Diane Herbort called upon many thoughtfully chosen ingredients for this dreamy confection: gathered, coiled, layered, and otherwise manipulated wire-edge ribbons; individual, clustered, and stacked buttons; seed and bugle beads worked in loops and dangles; dainty thread and silk ribbon embroidery; and a variety of silk ribbon, variegated floss, and velvet leaves. Use *your* favorite quilt-making genre or era as a starting point, and embellish your next project accordingly. For example, if the 1930s are your cup of tea, substitute pearl buttons, simple cotton embroidery threads, pastel gingham and grosgrain ribbons, bits of eyelet, and colorful rickrack for the more lavish, Victorian-style embellishments here.

Rubber stamping and a bit of ingenuity are the key factors employed by quilt artist Jan Smiley in her striking spin on the traditional basket. Unable to find the ready-made materials for the image she wanted, Jan created her own, basing them on sketches of anemones she found in a book on botanicals. Using an eraserlike carving medium called Nasco Safety-Kut and a linoleum carving tool with a #1 blade, she cut four rubber stamps that she combined with dark fabric inks and luscious batik fabrics to fashion custom flowers and foliage very much in keeping with her block's rich colors. Once stamped, the leaves and flowers were cut out, then layered and fused appliqué-style to the background. As a finishing touch, she added hand-beaded flower centers of clustered black seed beads. The strong colors and simple, woodblock-style stamped designs combine beautifully for a trendy, art nouveau flavor.

Altering with Embellishment

Initially surprised by the out-of-character color scheme presented to her, quiltmaker and master embroiderer Karen Phillips-Shwallon quickly rose to the challenge, simultaneously offering a virtual textbook on creative hand stitchery. She artfully tempers the bright hue of the background with complementary orangy red ruched flowers; stuffed coral daisies; and burgundy ribbon-stitched blossoms. Rosy bullion-stitch buds dance on stem-stitch stems, and tiny bullion stitches and seed bead buds nestle in the feathery long-stitch greenery. Clustered French knots, turkey work, and beading provide the sumptuous flower centers. As a finishing touch, Karen embellishes her basket with an undulating bow of hand-dyed, variegated, metallic-edge silk ribbon.

A BOUNTY OF BASKETS

Simple Elegance

Laura Heine, known for her creative threadwork, chose to fill her basket with a single, dramatic bloom, lavishly embellished with free-motion stitching. First, Laura fused the large pink petals and green leaves in place.

Second, using a standard-weight thread, she secured the edges of each appliqué with tiny stitches that intermittently extend toward the center of the applique—almost a random version of the buttonhole stitch. Then, using heavyweight YLI Jean Stitch thread, Laura introduced texture: striations and soft curves over the petals, serpentine veins in the leaves. A stitched leaf on the right echoes the appliquéd leaf and balances the overall design. A cluster of small ball beads makes the flower center a stronger focal point.

'Tis the Season

Baskets can be filled with many things besides flowers. Editor, author, and quilt designer Darra Duffy Williamson chose to go the holiday route, decking her basket with boughs of holly! Hand-dyed leaves in a suede-look cotton are secured with a delicate hand-embroidered feather stitch, leaving the edges free for dimension and texture. Glistening metallic bugle beads tip each pearl cotton vein, and cheery red buttons play the role of berries. For an added bit of holiday sparkle, narrow gold trim is laced around the basket handle (with the aid of a strong, large-eyed embroidery needle!). A gold raw-silk ribbon, threaded through a shiny gold buckle, and a bit of crocheted lace finish the piece. Why not take inspiration from this basket and embellish your designs with seasonal bounty? Think autumn leaves, winter twigs, birds' eggs or colorful Easter eggs in the spring, and summer fruits and vegetables.

The Quilter's
Problem Solver

The Coloring Book Approach

Problem	Solution
You're eager to begin developing your own ideas for embellishing traditional blocks, but you don't know where to start.	❑ If you'd like to try your hand at the basket block, simply photocopy and enlarge the diagram below at 200 percent twice, to produce a 10-inch square. Or reproduce it with a quilt design or graphics program on your computer. Color in the sketch, make multiple copies, and then audition various embellishments by laying or pinning them to the paper copies. See how many different embellishment options you can devise for a single pattern. ❑ Don't feel confined to the Basket block. Choose one of the others shown below, or refer to a block reference book for other examples. ❑ Include your quilting buddies in an embellishing adventure. For a creative group challenge, provide each member of your guild or group with the same pattern, such as the Basket, House, or Pine Tree. Encourage each person to embellish as desired. The blocks can be assembled and quilted for a unique fundraiser or a friendship quilt for an outgoing officer.

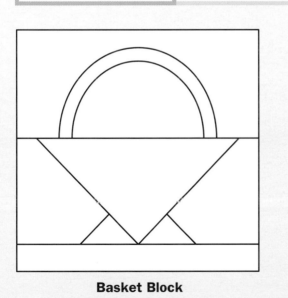

Basket Block

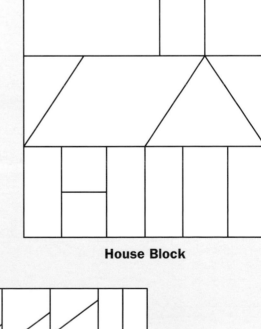

House Block

Patterns shown at 25%

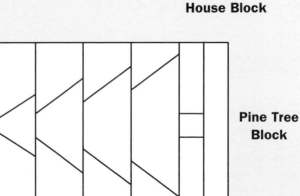

Pine Tree Block

Embellishments
Glossary

B

Beading. The technique of sewing beads (glass, metal, ceramic, semi-precious stone, wood, and other natural and synthetic materials) to fabric or other items by hand or machine.

Beading needle. An extra-long, fine, flexible needle designed for hand beading. Sizes commonly range from 10 to 15.

Beading thread. Strong, waxed or bonded thread that is intended especially for attaching beads to fabric.

Bobbin work. A machine stitching technique in which a decorative thread is wound onto the bobbin, and the stitching is done from the wrong side of the fabric. The stitched design is then on the right side.

Bugle beads. Thin, cylindrical beads available in a wide variety of colors and finishes. Bugle bead packages are marked with the length of the beads, usually ⅛ inch to 2 inches long.

C

Chenille needle. A hand-embroidery needle with a sharp tip and a long, oval eye; ideal for silk ribbon work.

Chenille stick. Fuzzy nylon threads along a length of wire, also known as a pipe cleaner. Bumpy chenille has sections that graduate from thick to thin.

Cording foot. A presser foot with a groove on the underside to accommodate cording or trim and, usually, a hole in the front to feed the trim through.

Cordonnet thread. The French name for topstitching thread. See *Topstitching thread.*

Couching. A method of securing decorative thread, yarn, ribbon, or another trim to a surface, either by hand or machine. The decorative thread is placed on the surface and stitched down with a zigzag, overcast, or other stitch.

D

Darning foot. A presser foot with a large opening at its base. The base may be circular or horseshoe-shaped, clear plastic or metal. Used for free-motion stitching or quilting with the feed dogs down or covered. The foot moves up and down with the needle, holding the fabric in place only when the needle is down.

Generic Darning Foot

Darning needle. A strong hand-embroidery needle with a large eye, ideal for use with bulkier threads and fibers such as wool.

Decorative stitching. Visible stitching added to fabric to create design lines, detail, and texture, rather than for joining pieces.

Decorative threads. Rayon, metallic, silk, wool, heavy cotton, or other unusual thread, yarn, or ribbon that may be sewn by machine or hand.

Dimensional appliqué. Appliqué in which the pieces rise above the surface of the background fabric. Fabric may be folded, gathered, or stuffed to achieve dimension.

Double needle. See *Twin needle.*

E

Embroidery needle. Hand or machine needle designed for use with flosses and metallic threads. The needle's large eye helps keep the thread from shredding.

F

Foil. A shiny, iridescent synthetic material, available in sheets, that can be adhered to fabric with an iron and fusible web.

Free-motion stitching. Machine stitching done with a darning foot on the machine and with the feed dogs lowered. This allows you to stitch in any direction you choose.

Fusible interfacing and fusible web. Materials that contain an adhesive activated by the heat of an iron. Fusible web is backed by paper and adheres two layers of fabric together. Fusible interfacing is used to stabilize or strengthen lightweight fabrics.

G

Gimp. An ornamental flat braid or round cord used as a trim, or as filling, such as for corded pintucks.

Grommet. A large metal eyelet such as those commonly found on shower curtains; also makes an innovative embellishment for quilts.

I

Inkset. A chemical solution used prior to the process of transferring images from a computer or photocopy to fabric. Inkset coats the fabric, making it receptive to the printer ink, so transfers are clearer and more permanent.

J

Jacquard ribbon. High-quality ribbon with woven-in designs, produced on a jacquard loom.

Jeans stitch thread. One of the thickest decorative threads used for machine embroidery, available in solid and variegated colors.

L

Lamé. Woven synthetic fabric that shines due to the presence of metallic fibers. While often used in garment making, this special-effect fabric can also create a dazzling accent in a quilt.

Light box. A glass or Plexiglas-topped box containing a bright light, ideal for tracing patterns for thread painting, appliqué, quilting, and so on.

Lingerie thread. A soft, supple, extremely fine nylon bobbin thread, ideal for machine embroidery, machine beading, and other machine stitchery.

M

Machine embroidery hoop. Like a traditional embroidery hoop, but adapted for machine work. Plastic and metal versions are thinner than traditional embroidery hoops, and wooden ones have a dip on one side, so you can slide it under a sewing machine needle without removing the needle.

Metallic thread. Decorative thread with a metallic coating; used for decorative machine stitchery and machine quilting.

Milliner's needle. A long, thin needle with a small, round eye; used for hand embroidery with finer silks and single-filament threads.

Monofilament thread. A very fine nylon thread available in clear or smoke. It can be used in machine beading or in machine quilting and appliqué, whenever stitches are intended to be invisible.

N

Nymo beading thread. Bonded nylon thread used for beading on fabric; available in a variety of colors and four sizes.

O

Open-toe presser foot. A sewing-machine foot with a cutaway design that allows a clear view of stitching. Use it to couch flat trims or to sew wide decorative stitches.

P

Passementerie. A fancy, textured trim that can be laid down in graceful curves. Varieties often feature coils, braids, or loops of strands covered with shiny rayon or polyester threads.

Pearl cotton. A heavy, silky-looking hand- or machine-embroidery thread, available in a variety of sizes and colors. The lower the thread number, the thicker the thread.

Photo transfer. The process of transferring an image from a black-and-white or color photo to a piece of fabric; it's a popular technique for making memory quilts.

Photo transfer paper. A heat-sensitive paper that's used with a photocopier to produce images you can iron onto fabric.

Pima cotton. A fine, tightly woven cotton fabric with a high thread count (200 threads per inch); it provides the clearest images for use with photo transfer techniques.

Pintuck. Traditionally, a tuck in the fabric formed when fabric is folded and stitched along the fold. Alternately, the *illusion* of a tuck, created by stitching on the right side of the fabric with a twin (or double) needle, a single bobbin thread, and a grooved pintuck foot.

Pintuck foot. A sewing machine foot with three to nine grooves on the underside, used with a twin (or double) needle. Intended for use when pintucking.

Prairie points. Decorative triangles made from folded fabric squares. Traditionally used as an inserted edge finish, prairie points may also be inserted in interior seams as an embellishment.

R

Ruching. A method of gathering, ruffling, or pleating. Ruched embellishments, often made from narrow strips of fabric or ribbon, are most often flower forms.

S

Sashing. Framing strips, also called lattice, that surround individual blocks or pieced units.

Seed beads. Tiny, versatile beads available in a variety of sizes and colors; the highest quality are glass.

Sew-through button. A button with two or four holes for attaching it to fabric.

Shank button. A button with a loop on the back for attaching it to fabric.

Shisha. A small mirrored embellishment, sewn in place with a buttonhole stitch.

Silamide thread. A nylon thread used for beading on fabric. Twisted rather than bonded, it resists shredding. Available in a variety of colors but only one size.

Six-strand embroidery floss. Strands of cotton thread in a wide range of colors, usually packaged in a skein; typically used for hand embroidery. Strands are most often separated and used two, three, or four at a time.

Stud. A usually shiny embellishment found in fabric and trim shops, with prongs that poke through the fabric and are flattened on the back to secure.

T

Tacking. A method of securing an item to fabric, or two fabrics together by means of minimal hand stitches.

Tear-away stabilizer. A nonwoven product pinned or basted to the wrong side of fabric to provide support and prevent stretching and puckering of the fabric when sewing decorative stitches. The stabilizer is removed (torn or cut next to the stitches) when the stitching is complete.

Thread count. The number of threads that lie in each direction on one square inch of fabric. Most quilter's

cottons have a thread count of about 60.

Threadpainting. The process of using a variety of colored and textured threads to create a detailed motif with dense free-motion machine stitches.

Tissue lamé. Lightweight synthetic fabric with a high metallic sheen.

Topstitching thread. A thick decorative thread ideal for machine embroidery; also called cordonnet thread.

Tulle. Often thought of as the fabric of choice for bridal veils, tulle is a lightweight, see-though, netting fabric.

Twin needle. A sewing machine needle that has one shaft but two shanks and eyes so that two parallel lines of stitching can be done simultaneously. Twin needles, also called double needles, are sold by size and by the distance (in millimeters) between the two needles.

W

Walking foot. A presser foot with a mechanism that works with the feed dogs to advance all layers of a quilt at the same rate, without shifting or puckering. Used for embellishing and quilting. Also called an even-feed foot.

Z

Zigzag stitch. A general grouping of machine stitches sewn with a needle swing from left to right.

G L O S S A R Y

Karen Kay Buckley's breathtaking quilts have graced the covers of many quilting magazines. She is the author of four books, including *Appliqué Basics: Flower Wreaths.* She has been quilting for over 15 years, teaching for 12, and was selected as Teacher of the Year in 1997 by *The Professional Quilter* magazine. Karen has over 250 quilts to her credit, and many have won major awards at regional and national competitions, including Best of Show at the 13th Quilters' Heritage Celebration in Lancaster, Pennsylvania. She resides in Carlisle, Pennsylvania, where she is very active in her local guild, the Letort Quilters.

Laura Heine is a designer, teacher, and quilt artist whose quilt One Fish, Two Fish, Red Fish, Blue Fish won the 1994 Bernina Award for best machine workmanship at the American Quilter's Society Competition in Paducah, Kentucky. She teaches for YLI Corporation, and her quilts are featured in their ads and brochures. Laura also designs fabrics for Kings Road Imports. Her latest lines include "Duet" (co-designed with Pat Smith) and "Ravissant." She is the author of *Color Fusion.*

Diane Herbort holds a degree in Fashion Design from the University of Cincinnati. She has written three books: *Gardening with Ribbons, Old Glories: New Lives for Treasured Textiles,* and *The Quiltwear Book.* Her work has been featured in numerous quilting and craft magazines, including *Quilter's Newsletter Magazine* and *American Quilter.* Her bead- and button-embellished King of Hearts quilt was part of the Smithsonian-sponsored exhibit *Art Quilts: Playing with a Full Deck* and is featured on the cover of the book on the exhibit. She has taught and judged at many major shows and seminars. She lives in Arlington, Virginia.

Alice Allen Kolb, internationally known teacher, designer, and author, has experiences ranging from university teaching to presenting seminars at international conferences. A regular contributor to quilting and other sewing-related publications, such as *Threads, American Quilter,* and *Bernina,* Alice is also the author of several books, including *Sashiko Made Simple, Needle and Thread,* and *Crazy Quilt by Machine.* She has both participated in and judged the AQS Fashion Show. Making her home in the Texas Hill Country, Alice thrives on the adventures found in her flower garden.

Diana Leslie developed a passion for quilting about 25 years ago. Applying her lifelong experience with sewing and other forms of needlework, she has since made many quilts for family, friends, and charities in the time left over from raising her own four children and many foster children. In her local quilt guild, Diana is recognized as an accomplished, versatile, and personable teacher; she has served her guild as an officer and chair of the annual quilt show, and she is active in the Mid-Atlantic Quilt Guild Network. Diana and her family live in Bucks County, Pennsylvania.

Linda McGehee is known worldwide for her award-winning books and patterns and for her techniques for achieving spectacular fabric manipulations. She travels extensively to lecture at trade and consumer conventions, at guilds and shops, and on television, sharing her methods for customizing fabrics to create unique surface textures. Her book *Simply Sensational Bags: How to Stitch and Embellish Handbags, Totes, and Satchels,* offers sensible and practical ideas for using texture to personalize bags. In addition to her books and popular pattern lines, Linda has also created three-dimensional designs for embroidery machines.

Karen Phillips-Shwallon has owned and operated *The Quilted Heart,* a teaching studio in Grindstone, Pennsylvania, for more than 15 years. She specializes in original-design needlework for all forms of embellishment, including dimensional embroidery, appliqué, crazy patchwork, and quilting. She has traveled extensively, teaching workshops designed to enhance the skill levels of her students. Karen recently designed a full-size quilt titled In Absence of Color. After winning numerous prizes at quilt shows throughout the United States, the quilt was donated to Children's Hospital of Pittsburgh, where it raised $17,000 at a gala fundraising auction.

Elizabeth Rosenberg has spent most of her life playing and working with fabric and thread, but when she made her first quilt in 1990, she was immediately enchanted by the process. She became obsessed with exploring the limits of her sewing machine's capabilities, using it to quilt, couch, embellish, and add flourish to her quilts. She teaches free-motion machine quilting and embellishment techniques, and through her company, Inventing Tradition, she also designs and distributes quilt patterns featuring images of Jewish tradition. She lives with her family in Yorktown Heights, New York.

Janet Rostocki is a graphic artist, illustrator, designer, publisher, and award-winning quilt artist whose works have appeared in numerous exhibitions and are held in private collections across the country. For 16 years, she has designed patterns and written and illustrated a popular line of books and patterns for quilts, home decor, and wearable art for her company, Summa Designs. She produced the original Jazzz clothing series and has written books on sewing, sashiko, embellishment, and wearables. Her most recent venture is a pattern line called Quiltings. She also writes and designs for several publishers and has taught and lectured at national seminars.

Diane Rode Schneck learned cross-stitch as a girl from her grandmother. By high school, she was embroidering jeans and shirts, and by college she'd discovered quilting. It was only a matter of time before she began to combine her passions. Diane is best known for her appliquéd and embellished quilts with humorous themes, and she is currently rediscovering her love of embroidery through crazy quilting. She lives in New York City, where she teaches a variety of quilting techniques. Under her pseudonym The Phabric Phantom, she also writes, lectures about, and leads shopping tours of New York's fabulous fabric and embellishment stores.

Jan Smiley started quilting in 1978 after seeing a Log Cabin block in a magazine. She's loved quilting ever since. Fabric selection and piecing are her favorite parts of the process. She has taught quiltmaking and fabric stamping classes for many years, and her colorful, innovative quilts have won awards at local, regional, and national shows. In the 1990s, Jan founded an international mail order fabric business, specializing in batik fabrics, which she ran with great success for 6 years. Jan lives with her family in Fort Mill, South Carolina.

Susan L. Stein began quilting in 1977, and has since made hundreds of wall pieces, liturgical hangings, garments, and bed quilts. A weaving exhibit in the 1980s opened her eyes to the possibilities of using embellishment to add depth and texture to flat surfaces. She enjoys using hand-dyed fabrics in her innovative interpretations of traditional patterns, as well as designing original pieces incorporating texture and vibrant colors. Susan teaches both locally and nationally and has owned two quilt shops in Minnesota, designed projects for many publications, written three books, and published many articles.

Carol Taylor is an internationally known, award-winning quilt artist whose art quilts grace the walls of several public venues and many private collectors. Her seemingly boundless energy is evident in the intensity with which she approaches her work, despite being a full-time sales recruiter. Her quilts are distinguished by the use of vibrant colors and striking contrasts, as well as heavy machine quilting and embroidery. Her accomplishments include having her quilts juried into Quilt National 2001 and 1999, winning major awards at the American Quilter's Society Show, and being named Best of Show in Made in NY 1999. She enjoys using both her own dyed fabrics and commercial silks.

Acknowledgments

Quilt Artists

Ginette Bourque, Power Surge, 2000, on page 3, details on page 70

Karen Kay Buckley, Flowers & Friends, 1997, on page 72; Floral Bouquet, 2000, page 79

Laura Heine, Look at My Wings, 2000, on page 60 and detail on page 63; Striped Quilt, 2000, on page 110

Diane Herbort, I've Got the Embellishment Blues, 2000, on pages 64–68

Janeene Herchold, Returning, 1998, on page 12; Hopscotch, 2000 and Sunflower, 1999, on page 69; Sunshine, 1999, on page 98 and detail on 99 (photo by Carina Woolrich)

Jean Wells Keenan, Token of Friendship, 1989, on page 81(photograph by Ross Chandler)

Alice Allen Kolb, Memory Garden, 1997, on page 42; A Silky Trail, 2000, on page 48

Diana Leslie, Lucy's Quilt 1999, details on pages 82 and 83

Linda McGehee, Sampler Vest, 1994, on page 56

Marguerite Malowitz, Undersea Scallops, 1988, on page 69

Janet Miller, Striped Homespun Quilt with Selvage Fringe, 2000, on page 112, from her book, *At the Heart of Folkart,* by the City Stitcher (see "Resources" on page 126)

Karen Phillips-Schwallon, Flower Basket, on page 12; Partridge in a Pear Tree, on pages 34 and detail on page 38; Red Penny Hen, on page 35 and detail on page 40; The Birds, on pages 38, 39, and 40; Eagle block, on page 39; A Little Bit of French, on pages 38 and 39 (see "Resources" on page 126)

Rachel Roggel, O' Daughters of Jerusalem, 1998, page 24 (photograph by Mason McCuddin)

Elizabeth Rosenberg, Golden Orbs, 1999, on page 14

Janet K. Rostocki, Vegetablesassy, 2000, on page 106 and detail on page 107; Fruity-Tooty, 2000, on pages 110 and 112

Joanie San Chirico, Palenque: Temple of the Sun, 2000, detail on page 30; Magic Carpet, 1999, on page 110; Nazca, 1999, on page 110 and detail on page 112

Diane Rode Schneck, Tea at the Ritz, 1999, on page 23; Log Cabin Cats, 2000, on page 23; The Opulent Quilt, in collaboration with Leslie Levison, 2000, details on pages 92, 94, and 95; The Cloth of Heaven, 1995, on page 93; A Cold Winter's Night, 1999, on page 94; The Elvis Album, 1995, on page 95; Night & Day, 2001, details on pages 95 and 96; A Child's Christmas in Cleveland, 1996, detail on page 96 (all quilts © Diane Rode Schneck)

Dora A. Serfass, Chick-a-dee-dee-dee, 1987, on page 23 (courtesy of AnnMarie and Brian Serfass)

Jan Smiley, Stamp Out Decaf, 2000, on page 50 and detail on page 54

Linda Dease Smith, Intuition and Light, 2000, on page 30

Sue Smith, My Painted Garden, 2000, on page 11

Susan Stein, Silk Crossroads, 2000, on page 102; Flights of Fancy, 2000, details on pages 100 and 101; Shades of Autumn, 1998, on page 101; Leaf Montage, 2000, on page 101

Carol Taylor, Coral Reef, 1999, on pages 4, 5, and 86

Polly Whitehorn, A Page from my Scrapbook, 1998, on page 80 and detail on page 83; A Bird in the Hand, 1999, on cover, page 26, and detail on page 94; Woodbridge Remembered, with round robin participation by Jeanine Love, Bobbie Brannin, and Virginia Bennetter, 1995, on page 6 and detail on page 84

Darra Duffy Williamson in collaboration with Linda Dease Smith, The Daily Bugle, 2001, on page 10

Thanks to Mary Helen Chiodo, Sonia Kobylarz, Eleanor Levie, Drinda Shelby, and Beth Wheeler for providing samples for this book.

Thanks to the NAMES Project Foundation for the use of the photograph by Paul Margolies of the Quilt DC '96 display of the AIDS Memorial Quilt on page 84.

Thanks to Mary Stori, Jane B. Garrison, and Penny Taylor-Wallace of TWE for sharing their knowledge and tips on embellishing. Thanks to Carol Britt of Batiks Etcetera & Sew What Fabrics, in Wytheville, Virginia, for providing the rubber stamps and Fabrico stamp pads on pages 50–54, and Diane Bartels for the hand and surface designed cotton and silk.

Fabrics & Supplies

American & Efird—Mettler threads, Signature machine-quilting threads

Bernina of America—Virtuosa 150 sewing machine

Fiskars—embroidery scissors, rotary cutters

Olfa—rotary cutters

Omnigrid—acrylic rulers, cutting mats

Plaid Enterprises—Plaid Decorator Block stamps, Glaze Vernis

Rowenta—Powerglide 2 iron

Sally Houk Exclusives—Specialty fibers for embroidery

Superior Threads—decorative threads

Resources

Artfabrik
664 W. Main St.
Cary, IL 60013
Phone: (847) 639-5966
Web site: www.artfabrik.com
Hand-dyed threads and bias tape, dyed cheesecloth

The City Stitcher
P.O. Box 413322
Dayton, OH 45441-0322
Phone: (937) 435-8875
Fax: (937) 433-0553
At the Heart of Folkart, *quilt designs by Janet Miller, directions for the fringed quilts on page 112*

Clotilde
B3000
Louisiana, MO 63353
Phone: (800) 772-2891
Web site: www.clotilde.com
Pressing sheets, Inkset, photo transfer sheets, fabric markers, stilettos, Clover Bias Tape Maker, No-Fray, fusibles and stabilizers, hand and sewing machine needles, decorative threads

Dharma Trading Company
P.O. Box 150916
San Raphael, CA 94915
Phone: (415) 456-7657
E-mail: catalog@ dharmatrading.com
Web site: www.dharmatrading.com
Inkset, Jacquard fabric paints, 200 thread-count fabric for photo transfer

Fiberworks, Inc.
1310 24th St., W
Billings, MT 59102
E-mail: laurah@fiberworks-heine.com
Web site: www.fiberworks-heine.com
Pattern for "Look at My Wings" on page 60

Diane Herbort Designs
3532 S. 16th Street
Arlington, VA 22204
E-mail: Herbort@aol.com
Trims used in the quilt shown on pages 64–68

M&J Trimmings
1008 Sixth Ave.
New York, NY 10018
Phone: (212) 391-9072
Web site: www.mjtrim.com
Trims, braids, ribbon, embroidered patches, jewels, sequins, studs, beads

Mill Hill Beads
Gay Bowles Sales
3930 Enterprise Dr.
P.O. Box 1060
Janesville, WI 53547
Phone: (608) 754-9466
Web site: www.millhill.com
Beads, novelty buttons

Laura Murray
5021 15th Ave., S
Minneapolis, MN 55417
Phone: (612) 825-1209
E-mail: lmurray128@aol.com
9" × 12" foil sheets

The AIDS Memorial Quilt
NAMES Project Foundation
310 Townsend St., Suite 310
San Francisco, CA 94107
Phone: (415) 882-5500
Fax: (415) 882-6200
E-web site: www.aidsquilt.org

Karen Phillips-Shwallon
The Quilted Heart
258 Stone Church Rd.
Grindstone, PA 15442-9730
Phone: (724) 246-9076
Fax: (724) 246-0512
E-mail: quilthrt@stargate.net
Original embroidery patterns

Sulky of America
3113 Broadpoint Dr.
Harbor Heights, FL 33983
E-mail: info@Sulky.com
Web site: www.sulky.com
Decorative threads and stabilizers, including Sulky Heat Away and Totally Stable

TWE Beads
P.O. Box 55
Hamburg, NJ 07419-0055
Phone: (973) 209-1517
Fax: (973) 209-4471
E-mail: rp@twebeads.com
Web site: www.twebeads.com
Beads, Nymo and Silamide threads, beading supplies